CLIMBING the ROCK WALL

CLIMBING the ROCK WALL

Surviving a Career in Public Education

Barbara D. Katz-Brown

Library of Congress Control Number:		2013915857
ISBN:	Hardcover	978-1-4836-9348-4
	Softcover	978-1-4836-9347-7
	Ebook	978-1-4836-9349-1

This book was printed in the United States of America.

Rev. date: 09/19/2013

To order additional copies of this book, contact:
Xlibris LLC
1-888-795-4274
www.Xlibris.com
Orders@Xlibris.com
138583

CONTENTS

This book is dedicated to my loving husband Steve Brown, who never stopped encouraging me to try various administrative positions within a centrally isolated school district in upstate New York, no matter how the schedule disrupted our daily life and no matter how much I complained.

Steve held me when I cried, encouraged me when I was shafted by my colleagues, and lastly, believed that, given the chance, I was always the best person to make the changes needed for the success of the students.

This book is also dedicated to *all* new teachers. Hang in there and try to make the system work with you. Our country's children are at stake.

The cover is a photo of the Torres de Serranos in Valencia, Spain. It was taken by the author who was most impressed by the smoothness of the walls of the towers. Serrano Gates is one of the twelve gates that were found along the old medieval wall in Valencia meant to protect the ancient city. Valencia was founded as a Roman colony in 138 BC.

Climbing the Rock Wall is a metaphor for trying to achieve a successful career in public education in the United States. The smoother the wall to climb, the more difficult it will be to reach the top—same in the world of public education.

PREFACE

There are many reasons I felt compelled to write a book about my experiences in public education. People say that if you are addicted to something, the first way to overcome it is to admit your addiction. In public school education, at least in New York State, many erroneous practices need to be brought to the forefront. The public has been addicted to rhetoric that proposes change, as if the word *change* or *reform* means "better." The list of things that need to be transformed in order to guarantee each student a quality education is even more extensive than I can begin to describe in this book, but I can start a discussion.

For those who believe everything is working just fine and should remain status quo, I would challenge them to explain why so many students still drop out of high school in this country or why children today are having such a hard time finding and keeping a job. We need to adjust both our curriculum to reflect the technological/vocational needs of the future and the models of delivery of that information. We need to catch a child's interest in the language arts, science and math much like catching a butterfly—and guide that student toward investigation. The current curriculum and methodologies embedded in standards from the pre-kindergarten years through twelfth grades in this country squash any interest in learning for many children. Finally, we need to remember that not every child learns in the same way and that we must alter tactics so they become aligned with the learning style or cultural influences of the student.

There is a huge call for a thorough overhaul of the educational system, known as the reform movement today and as soon as possible in order to compete in this global economy. However, what is asked in the current basics of the reform movement is much of the *same old, same old* but organized differently. It is not enough. Look toward the state of Pennsylvania, which has some great ideas about education as do countries like Japan, Korea, Sweden, and China. We should look out and observe what kind of teaching and learning happens in schools in other developed nations. Not to say we have not done this in the past as the *Whole Language* reading movement from New Zealand swept the country in the eighties. Unfortunately, the United States publishers went crazy printing little books without conducting proper studies about the effectiveness of the materials.

In the great state of New York, for example, we have to begin to think out of the New York State Regents box or any of the states' old leadership ways and challenge each board to hire superintendents of schools who are true lifetime members of their community. We must grow our own leaders from within each community. What a great example for our own students!

Real institutional change is required to be able to address the skills of our students in this millennium. Obviously, courses in finance and vocational training are only two subjects that need to be added. An increase in the number of school days and the length of the school day will need to part of the theoretical construct so that the United States can remain a competitive nation. We have only to look at what other countries have done to guarantee the success and future employment of their students. We can no longer operate on a 180-day-farming seasonal schedule of classes, and our focus needs to be adjusted. All children learn best with more practice, and we need more time with all of them. It will be costly for our nation to add school days, but just as costly to keep hiring people from other countries to do the work.

I have been influenced by leaders in education such as Harold Gardner, Ruby Payne, and Jonathan Kozol. I have also been influenced by the practices of many psychologists such as B. F. Skinner, Jean Piaget, and Elisabeth Wiig of Boston University.

The practicing administrators I admire most were not always famous, but they were good at their jobs. They include Roger Buell, an elementary principal (now deceased), and Ronald Acerra, a middle school principal (now retired). There were a few other impressive leaders during my thirty-three years, three months, and three days employed in a centrally isolated public school system in Upstate New York, but these men demonstrated leadership through action, knowledge, and trust. Ironically, there were few women whom I could call true mentors or whom I could trust in the education business. I learned to emulate the way the best professionals in many disciplines solved problems, directed effective positive change, and spoke with children, parental guardians, administrators, teachers, and staff.

I decided not to address my experiences with the teachers' union in these essays. I have only had positive experiences with the support of my colleagues, and I gave back by being the membership chair of my local union and on the negotiating team when our contract needed to be renewed. I was a member of the teachers' union even though I held administrative jobs because of the leave of absence from my tenured position loophole that allowed me a foot in each pool, wary of wading in too deeply; I was always on the side of the teachers, no matter what occurred. I believe that if an administrator could always be on the side of the teachers, life would be so much more pleasant on a daily basis. I don't know what pill a teacher takes when that teacher becomes an administrator, but I did not swallow that pill and therefore, I confess to being a teacher supporter.

While some may say a book such as this is only a memoir and not worthy of distribution, I think that belief is short sighted. This book is intended for every new person considering public education as a career or for someone entrenched within a public school system and feels no one is listening. Both audiences need to know the game in order to survive. Politics exist in every workplace and phase of life. The politics within a public school system in any state in the United States can kill you—cause an early death—or you can learn how to make the system work for you based upon the experiences I share within this book.

I'd love for the regents in the state of New York, the chancellor of education in the United States, the governor of the state of New York, and Oprah Winfrey to read this book so they may recognize the problems that I have outlined and begin a real dialogue about what is needed to fix the public school system in the United States for all children.

I do not think of leadership as a position. I don't think of leadership as a skill. I think of leadership as a relationship.

—Philip J. Quigley (former CEO, Pacific Bell)

THE WHY

"Why didn't *you* get the job as the principal?" "Why didn't they hire *you?*" Every time someone asked me those questions, I would respond with two statements. Usually, the first response was, "The most qualified people aren't always hired." The second response was, "Ask the superintendent."

Working over thirty-three years, three months, and three days of experience in a centrally isolated Upstate New York school district has provided many, many stories. What inspired me to write this combination memoir and guide for beginners in the educational system was not getting those positions in educational administration I had coveted earlier in my career.

Climbing the Rock Wall is the written result of years of frustration for *not* getting the rewards (positions) I thought I deserved after studying and working so hard. When I was a Girl Scout, I had been taught to follow the directions, to follow through with projects, and to be respectful at all times. The result of playing nice would be advancement or, at least, a badge. Unlike the Girl Scout mantra, a day in public school education is fraught with dramatic stories involving children and adults that even the writers of the best TV soap opera or reality show of this century could not create, and so, as is often the case, no badge or recognition of effort is received from anyone. Until I began to write my essays, no one had ever dared reveal the nitty-gritty of the educational system as it truly is in real life. Through my essays, the general public will be provided some sense of what life is like in the public schools for an ambitious woman.

Climbing the Rock Wall combines my compiled knowledge of the institutional practices and systems of schools in the United States. It includes my lifelong study of normal child development and the role of parental responsibilities within the educational environment. The work is based upon current research in the fields of behavioral science, educational theory, and years of experience in the field (classroom).

Topics I cover throughout the book range from what teachers really talk about in the staff lounge to trading administrators from one school district to the next, like horse trading in the western frontier. Some essays are longer than others, and some are more controversial. Some essays reflect political views: others are more anecdotal.

Who is my potential audience? My audience should be every parent with a student in the public schools, every director of every state education department, every teacher who aspires to be an administrator, every public school administrator, and every person in this country who wants to know what goes on behind the closed schoolroom doors.

Why didn't I get to be a principal? You'll have to read the book.

KEYS

Mr. Miller used to walk down the hallway jiggling his keys. We always knew when he was coming, so my class of sixth graders would always look like they were working when he rounded the corner. He taught us some of the time and gave us daily assignments to work on independently. Then he would walk the halls as the principal of the school. He walked the halls a lot, jiggling those keys. Sometimes he sang and jiggled. Sometimes he whistled and jiggled. Mostly, he just jiggled those keys. And the class always knew when he was coming back so we could stop copying each other's papers. I learned math in the sixth grade by copying answers others had already completed. No shame, just like the kids in the class, I learned how to "share."

At the time, I thought principals were the smartest people in the entire world and, by being smart, you were then chosen to become a principal. I always wondered what Mr. Miller knew about teaching that the teachers did not know. He probably knew all the names of the governors in the country. He at least knew all the football players at Rutgers University because he frequently named them for us. I had heard that Mr. Miller knew where the local bar was, but that was probably just gossip. Teachers often talked about him in the teachers' room because I heard his name mentioned when I had to deliver notes to teachers in the staff room.

I was Mr. Miller's pet. He used to call me Kitty because of my last name, Katz. My mother was a third-grade teacher in the school, so he had a personal relationship with our family, as it seemed. I did have the honor of running lots of errands for him throughout the elementary school day, and I learned how to listen behind closed doors and next to open doors when an adult was speaking. (This is one skill that has come in handy throughout my life).

In my youth I thought one definitely had to be a man to be a principal. This was 1961, and the word *administrator*, in my mind, meant the same thing as the superintendent of my grandparents' apartment building in Brooklyn—you know, the family that lived in the basement near the garbage cans of the buildings in Brooklyn, New York, where my grandparents lived. The superintendent or "super" lived with his family in the smelliest part of the building. I decided, as any child would, that this was not such a good job. Although Mr. Miller was a principal, not a super, he walked the halls with the super whenever the man was in the building, and as a principal (in my sixth-grade view of life), he got to do whatever he wanted to do whenever he wanted. The job of principal seemed to be something I would want to do someday. Walking around and telling people what to do was my complete understanding of the duties of the position as principal of an elementary school.

Mr. Miller had the only radio in the school in his office, which was on all the time during the school day. One could hear newscasts and music drift out into the hallway as we passed his office on the way in and out of the building for recess, lunch, or when we needed to find him for a message from a teacher. Long before cell phones, each classroom had an intercom, which was not private, so sensitive messages to teachers via paper was the only way to communicate directly. As kids, we relished the idea of leaving our classroom to deliver something important. Kids feel the same way today.

Mr. Miller was the only man, besides the custodian, in the entire school. The rest of the teachers were women, including my mother. All my mother's friends were my teachers from kindergarten until the first half of the sixth grade when I moved out of the school district. I received various privileges as a result of being the Pet, but on the downside, my mother knew everything about my day even before I got home from school.

Mrs. Katz was one of the new elementary teachers in the school, and her colleagues quickly took her under their wing, just like hens in a henhouse. By the way, many of the teachers also had henhouses in their backyards at the time. In fact, one of the henhouse-owning teachers became my teacher for two grades. Mrs. Rhodes was my first-grade teacher and my fourth-grade teacher. She was also Jewish and, with her husband, Jerry, owned a house with a huge chicken coop. This was rural, at the time, central New Jersey. Farms were still prevalent.

Plots of land were being sold to developers, and my parents bought our pink house on what was a blueberry farm. My mother and father grew up in apartments in New York, Massachusetts, and Ohio but mostly in Brooklyn, New York. When my parents bought their first house in Old Bridge, they tried to landscape the property. Mrs. Rhodes gave them a tree to plant in the front yard, and my mother planted some bushes. This was the first time our immigrant family had owned land to plant anything anywhere.

Mrs. Rhodes would often invite the other teachers over for coffee at her house after school, and my mother would bring me along. I'd sit in the room next door and read, color in my coloring book, or check out the smelly birds in the henhouse. I was scared of them, but I wanted to see an egg come out. Mrs. Rhodes would send me out the door with an egg basket, but the thought of putting my little hand underneath those birds never happened. I figured out that if I just waited, an egg would roll out to me, but it never did. The egg-waiting thing gave me something to do as the teachers discussed all the bad and poor kids in the school, rumors about the principal, etc. It was my first introduction to serial public-school soap-opera life.

I learned at an early age that teachers don't discuss the latest educational theory in the teachers' room or at their houses. The teachers during the 1950s followed the teachers' manuals with the answers printed in them. They wrote out sentences to copy on a piece of paper from the board and required the students to "fix" the grammar and punctuation. Many teachers wrote the math problems on the board to copy and solve, always showing your work. A no-frills education.

Each elementary teacher taught art and physical education. The music teacher came around to each classroom with a cart loaded with books and percussion instruments. The pianos on wheels were reserved for the kindergarten classrooms.

Every day in my morning / half-day kindergarten class, the teacher would hand out a mimeographed purple worksheet to color. Some kids sniffed the paper because they liked the smell. I didn't do that because I knew that the fat teacher kept the papers under her arm while she walked down the hallway, and no way was I going to sniff her underarm odor. No way. Of course, I never told anybody because they wouldn't believe it. I saw her stick those papers under her arm coming down the hallway, and the body odor would have been the discriminating smell, not the alcohol. There were seventy-five kids in my kindergarten class in 1957. We marched around the room as the teacher played the piano. We sang songs, colored endless BO / alcohol smelly mimeos. We cut and pasted endless pieces of paper, learned the alphabet, and counted to one hundred. Kindergarten. One half day. Big deal. I already knew all this stuff. I did get an *unsatisfactory* on my report card because I left my hanky at home several times. After that, my mother pinned one to my hanky holder on my dress each day. There was no physical room to do anything else in that classroom. So much for public education and hanky holders in the '50s. Do they even make those things anymore?

Mr. Miller was my first school administrative role model. I figured that if I could be a principal, I'd get a lot of keys, have a good parking space, roam the halls to see what is going on, and everyone would know I was smart. Besides, being smart was much more important in my family, and in this potential job as a principal, I could do anything I wanted to do all day long and have a radio in my office. The role of an elementary principal changed quite a bit as I was going to discover in the upcoming years, but some aspects of the job remain the same today.

ANECDOTE

The major thing a student wants more than anything else is attention. Attention from adults is coveted all day, every day. The method a student of any age may use to gain that attention can range from doing kind things for the teacher to throwing a chair at another student. Students who have frequent disciplinary issues in any grade are craving notice by an adult of any kind for both positive behaviors and negative behaviors. I will try to outline, in various anecdotes throughout this book, some of the behaviors I have observed children engaging in during the school hours so the public understands some of the pressures within an institution for young children and young adults.

Let me start with a story about a student I'll name Ben. Ben was a ninth-grade student who refused to go to social studies despite supports put into place in the classroom, such as an extra special education teacher in the classroom to adapt the regular curriculum to students with disabilities. This practice in education is called inclusion. Ben preferred the associate principal's (AP's) office to his social studies classroom, so he would do anything to get kicked out of the classroom. He banged desks, refused to cooperate with the teacher's directives, would not stop talking when the teacher spoke, and created havoc in the classroom every day. Ben would sit in the AP's office, my office, for most of the instructional day doing nothing but listening to the business I had to do as AP.

One day I sat down next to him on my couch and asked him how he was going to learn the material like algebra in math and about countries in social studies outside of the classroom, in my office. He had no answer. I suggested Ben try some things, like growing up and taking responsibility and reporting to me each day after school about one thing he had learned in each class. He started the first day, shyly, standing at my door, blurting out "ordinals," and then every day, he would find me at the buses before he boarded his to go home and yelled something out. "Compost, fracture lines, bicoastal waterways, hypothesis . . ." Every day I saw him, I told him how much more mature he acted and appeared and thanked him for reminding me about the vocabulary each subject area he is receiving instruction in during the day. Every minute more of the school day Ben spent in the classroom increased his chance of graduating from high school. Ben was in the ninth grade, in his first year of high school, and the pendulum could have swung in a completely different direction. After a few months, Ben stopped coming into the AP's office, except to brag about getting good grades and trips he could take with his classmates. My reward to him was simple. I had him come back, and I reminded him of my initial question: how he was going to learn the material like algebra and about countries in social studies outside of the classroom, in my office. Ben responded this time: "I guess I didn't have to do weird things so I would get kicked out of the class." What Ben really meant was that he would receive more attention from adults when he cooperated.

Bingo! Sometimes a little attention from an adult helps a kid figure out what they need to do to become more successful.

THE FIRST PRINCIPAL

The very first principal I remember working for was in my first position as a speech therapist in a little town in Connecticut. The town looked like the television soap opera popular in the '60s called *Peyton Place* and was a small school district. The superintendent was a former superintendent in the school district I grew up in while a student in New Jersey. This is probably why he hired me fresh out of college with a plan that I had to work and get my master's degree from the neighboring university, the University of Connecticut, at night. The superintendent gave me a personal tour of the campus and hired me on the spot. The total time of the interview was three hours from start to finish, including a tour of all the school buildings by the super himself, and no committee was needed in order to make a decision.

I was the speech and language therapist for the entire district, and I split my days in three different buildings between the grades kindergarten to high school. In that school district, the principal I remember most was a young man in the grade school filled with older, mature women. I didn't interact with him very much, but he came to my apartment for a little party I had for my coworkers. I had only a few chairs to sit on, but I vacuumed, polished, and bought food for the event. On the night of the party, it was very warm, and I didn't have air-conditioning in my apartment. Mr. Principal sat on one of the chairs I had polished in the afternoon, and the polish on the back of the wood chair bled onto his yellow Lacoste shirt. He reacted with humor, and I offered to replace the shirt. It was one of my most embarrassing moments with an administrator.

When I left the district at the end of the first year, it was to pursue my master's degree. UConn, it turned out, would only let me matriculate in the master's degree speech program as a full-time day student. I had talked my way into one night course on adult aphasia with some famous professor, but that was all I could do. I couldn't understand how a state university could be so rigid, especially if they really wanted continuing education for the professionals in the state.

I never really interacted with that principal again. I just remember what I had done to his shirt.

THE RED DRESS

When I first applied for a position in a centrally located, isolated school district in New York State, it was a very warm day in August. The interview room was not air-conditioned in the board of education building, and the people sitting as interviewers were clearly uncomfortable, dabbing their brows with Kleenex and waiting to finish the day. This was my first experience interviewing for anything in this school district and my only experience interviewing with a committee of professionals in my field.

There were three speech therapists, two women and one man, who served as the chairman of the group. I knew the man because I had volunteered to work with a student with a stuttering disability at one of the middle schools in the same district while I attended graduate school. In the past, my efforts had helped the department to cover the students at no cost to the taxpayers. The chairman had been my supervisor and was very helpful and grateful at the same time. No one else had wanted to work with this student besides me. I had wanted to work to accumulate required hours in the area of dysfluency and to demonstrate my ambition early in my career.

After six months of teaching in Connecticut, I had some viable experience under my belt, and I wasn't as green as I could have been at the interview. Also in my favor was the fact that one of the women's husbands taught at the same college and in the same department as the man I was dating at the time. I felt sure of myself and knew that I had a good chance of getting this three-quarters time position in the district. How hard could this be?

Still, I was a bit nervous. All the questions were related to speech therapy, and I answered with ease. I had received excellent training in my undergraduate and graduate programs in the field, as well as student teaching experience in two placements—one of which was as an elementary speech therapist, and the other placement was at an adult psychiatric center.

The committee asked about my student teaching and about my duties in my former job in Connecticut. As the youngest person at the table, this group was trying to see if I fit into their family of therapists. No matter what position I had been interviewed for in the past, I had always gotten the job, so I was actually looking forward to speaking about myself (as many Aries women do, I am told).

When I returned home, I changed out of the dress I was wearing and realized that my entire body was red. The dye from the dress had bled onto my underwear and my skin. It took some scrubbing in the shower to get the dye off and I should have seen this as some kind of warning. I should have considered what this meant if I had gotten the job. I must have been more nervous than I thought I was at the interview.

The chairperson called me later that afternoon thanking me for interviewing and letting me know that I had the position if I wanted it. I would be the fourth therapist in the district and would be responsible for covering two elementary schools, all the prekindergarten programs, and the Catholic school. Not bad for a three-day-a-week position, just impossible. It didn't matter that a nice Jewish girl from New Jersey may be working in the Catholic school or that I still needed to find additional employment to supplement my income. I had won a position in this centrally isolated Upstate New York school district and was chosen by my professional peers. What could be more exciting?

I threw the red dress into the garbage and vowed to tell others never to wear a red dress on a warm day to an interview for any position without washing it first. Of course, protocol today would say that it is verboten to wear red to an interview.

LIFE IN THE TRENCHES

Today begins another summer vacation. Life in the trenches of a school district will remain with me for another week or so until I do not have to think about the characters in this reality drama. The superintendent, director of human resources (there's a joke), or the assistant to the superintendent, various principals, and a few directors are not coming with me to the New Jersey beach. These are the layers of soil I must deal with every day, and I don't want them in my shell-based, sandy vacation.

I would like to pitch a series for a reality television show like *Undercover Boss* to see who could survive a few months as a public school district employee. The positions would range from custodian to superintendent, and the board would decide who contributes the most to a group of kids that are failing in high school. Let's see who has the most success with these students. The criteria could be the high school diploma. I would ask that each of these adults go to work every day and then come home to the student. In this experiment, the needed certification field is leveled, and people have to switch jobs. Let's see how the folks at the top of the school echelon consider the life/job of the bus driver or the bus aide at summer school as the temperatures climb in July.

Does a superintendent making $165,000 a year and a free car to use really understand the powerless of an untenured cafeteria aide's life? How would she feel if he/she had to stand there every day at lunch watching children behaving badly? A bullhorn is not included with the paycheck for the average lowly, minimal-wage worker.

Here is an example of the waste of the taxpayers' money and life in the trenches. A person performs a specific job for fifteen years and does it well. She makes daily mail deliveries, takes care of the mail in the mailroom, exchanges pleasantries with everyone she delivers to in some way, and keeps us informed as to the roads in bad weather. The superintendent cuts her position, and Sally (not her real name) has to apply for another position; a custodial position that pays $14 an hour less is the only one offered to her. The position will be covered by building and grounds now, and this woman was forced to interview and then accept a position as a custodian or have no job while under appeal with her union.

Meanwhile, she is demoralized and feels threatened. Then the board of education approves a 3% raise for the superintendent based on performance. The raise would have more than covered the difference in this woman's salary even if she had to take another position.

Or let's talk about the teaching assistant who has had no formal training when hired but will be dealing with students with behavioral or emotional disabilities. We hired her to be a one-to-one aide for an elementary student. The aide had an undergraduate degree in psychology. That's it. The first full day on the job, she gets punched and kicked. She comes back the second day and spends all day with the student in an in-school suspension room. There is *no* district training for this position because the district "can't afford it." Then she is guided by the social worker after the student has a meltdown. The third day (yes, she came back), the student spat at her and ran out the front door of the school with a number of people trailing behind him, including the aide. Now, this is a complex student with many problems. In this case, the student's academic placement in a regular school needs to be reexamined, but again, we put the least trained person with the neediest students. The aide was making minimum wage at thirty-five hours a week. The chance of the student achieving academic success at this stage was limited.

Next, we have to discuss life in the trenches for the average elementary teacher. In this district that is centrally isolated in Upstate New York, the demands on a teacher's life are great. The community consists of world-renowned professors, children transplanted here from New York City, and the rural poor who have lived in the area for most of their lives. The class the teacher teaches may also be composed of a number of students whose first language is not English either owing to father/mother status or student status or refugee status and they have come to our fair city for safe haven. The school hours are 8:00 AM to 2:20 PM. It is not a long-enough day for the students, but for the teacher under the current systems, it is way too long.

My own father's concept of my mother's day as a third-grade teacher was a bit off the mark. He thought my mother sat at her desk all day and taught up to thirty-five children in her third-grade class. He could never understand why she needed to go to sleep at nine o'clock in the evening or why she used her preparation times to mark papers while the students were at art class or music class. He did see her mark report cards, but he never realized just how much she did.

The average teacher today does not leave school as soon as the students do. She comes in early to prepare, stays late to prepare, comes to school on the weekend to prepare, and brings work home every night. Many teachers do home visits and now maintain homework web pages. Most of the teachers I know who provide quality-first instruction put in at least a ten-hour day on the job and at least five hours of the weekends and holidays. It is a different ten hours of the day. At least six of the hours you are not alone but teaching. So sitting at a desk with a nice cup of coffee, checking your e-mail, and planning how you will complete that project for the day or going to a meeting with more coffee and donuts is not the life of a public school teacher. Once you set foot in the doorway, you are "on" until you drive out of the parking lot (if there is one) at the end of the day.

And children are messy, snotty, and dirty, and some even smell badly. Lice and ringworm, scabies, and colds are all part of the job. Children are certainly not hazard-proof either and have to be watched constantly so as not to inflict pain on themselves and others. I always laugh when parents say that they don't know how to volunteer since they don't do crafts or whatever. I have always invited them to come to lunch and sit at a table and have a conversation with a few children or come to the playground and teach a game that you loved as a child. This is the best way to volunteer at a school. It does not require one to attend PTA meetings or anything. Forget baking cupcakes; just be a parent in presence.

Life in the trenches can be very rewarding when there is enough positive support from central office administration, help from the community, and pride in one's school. Or it can be a living hell.

GIGS BEGET GIGS

Common sense tells you that experience in one area of education would make a better administrator in the public schools. If you have taught at a specific grade level, then you know the curriculum, the standards, and which outcomes in student performance the community desires. A lack of experience at that grade level would then suggest a lack of basic knowledge in those areas described.

Therefore, one would believe that to hire someone whose experience is limited or nonexistent in that area would be foolish if other applicants for the position had knowledge in those subjects.

In my career in this centrally isolated New York State school district, this has not been the custom. This is because of the politics involved in the hiring process. The rewards of special positions to people who have done what was requested from the top of the institution continue with "appointed" positions. Similar jobs and titles are available to some more than others. Positions are advertised, changed, or never filled if only local candidates apply. The thrust may be to hire minority candidates, but the lack of support once in the position is not well documented, and the administrators or teachers leave our area after a short while. This is a major problem, which could be solved by growing our own teachers and administrators.

I once worked with a principal who had volunteered to do everything from serving as president of her local union to construction leader of a playground on weekends. She served on more committees than one person could have imagined—all at the same time. She had no life outside of the district, and her family surely suffered. All she wanted was a position within the central office. She will not be able to advance from within this school district now perhaps because her activities were perceived as a threat to the super. This woman has gone as far as she can go within the district, and unless she looks elsewhere, this will be her light in life—as a principal in a rural school forever. This is not a bad position, and many people aspire to do just this, but this woman was ambitious, and our district dashed any hopes she had of being a district leader.

The vision of the head leader (super) of a school district is shaped by many factors. He or she hires the people that will fit into the vision. One would hope that the leader has the information he/she would need to know what each school needs in terms of leadership. To make a good match, the educational leader needs to know his/her schools and community. This is the challenge of the superintendent who comes into a community from somewhere else.

By being a member of the country club, the yacht club, the Rotary club, and nothing else does not prepare a super to understand the community. He/she must be willing to attend a church/synagogue/mosque service of *all* the faiths, shop in all types of grocery stores, and attend all the plays, concerts, and sports events in order to become familiar with the needs of the community. Of course, walking around each building in the district would help as well, not just on the first days of school.

So the challenge for the new educational administrative intern is to obtain a placement where the administrator is skilled in management and politics. It helps to follow someone with knowledge of what should be taught at that level, but obviously, this is not the topic priority. Reading articles, books, and research in the area of organizational management is far more beneficial to running a school district than a thorough knowledge of curriculum in the beginning. By taking as many different assignments as possible, some related to what you want to do and some differently related, the curriculum vitae is constructed, and the experiences in administration should start piling up. You should work in grades prekindergarten through the twelfth grade if you want to understand a district. You should attend as many board of education meetings as possible and make nice with all the bigwigs.

Musicians say that if you substitute for the regular player of a band or orchestra on any given night, you may just *become* the regular player. So don't turn down a "gig" because it is only as a substitute. These spontaneous opportunities build more contacts, involve more players, and could lead to learning something new. The road of life is filled with interesting turns if you dare to take them.

Supposedly, if you take more educational administrative posts, you will get more posts in the future, which is why the game involves moving from one post every few years, like the game of chess. If this strategy does not work, then doing something in the community that involves leadership will exercise the same skills. It is my official belief that, in the end, it does not matter what you did in your career. In a nursing home, the school custodian patient could be parked in his wheelchair next to the patient who was the district superintendent of schools. Whoever smells the worst may be changed first. Title does not matter at this point in life.

As Eleanor Roosevelt observed, "No one can hurt you without your consent."

SUMMER DAYS

I always figured that I could bypass having to be a summer school principal and obtain a position as a principal. The way this actually played out was probably stranger than strange. So before I had a stint as an associate principal at a middle school, I applied to be the summer school principal and didn't get the job (of course). There were two candidates, and I guess I just didn't charm the skirt off the administrator who was doing the interviews. I really didn't want to do the job that year anyway. I'd buy myself one more summer at the beach, and it worked out to be just as well for my family.

The following spring, I applied again to be the summer school principal. By this time, the woman I had interviewed the summer before had been booted out of the district for mysterious reasons—a common occurrence recently in this district—and another person was at the summer school position-hiring helm. Actually, I had hired this newer woman for a teaching position in our district, and now she was interviewing me. Just goes to show you that the power one has on Tuesday can change by Thursday afternoon.

So after a list of questions, I was going to be the summer school principal for three consecutive summers. My own children's college tuition bills now had a chance. I became the summer school principal, grades kindergarten through eighth, which would be housed in three district buildings, half days in the morning, 250 kids, two meals during the time in school, "bused out" over 166 district miles for a total of four weeks. Put this program together in three months and we have an expert summer school! Yeah. This was pre-cell phone days and pre-Internet availability days for all employees, so everything needed to coordinate the program was done by hand. My family helped by writing the bus information on little postcards to send to parents.

I had been to a number of camps in my life. I had put conferences and conventions together. No problem. What I didn't count on was supervising a morning program in three locations with miles and miles between. On one hand, when I got into my car, the air-conditioning and peace and quiet was amazing.

The teachers were district employees and veteran summer school teachers. My supervisor and I had a slightly different vision of what the morning should look like that year. Apparently, many of the teachers were accustomed to long walks in the woods with the students so they could discuss and then write about their experience. I had enjoyed this transcendental type of approach to the teaching of writing before in my career, and it was not really effective. You have to actually teach children how to write by constructing sentences on paper. Long walks can be inspiring, but they are not going to show a student where to add an adverb.

Now, these children were remedial and needed to have more time writing and less time walking. This did not go over well at first. The teachers were comfortable and accustomed to their ways in the summer.

We began with a three-day workshop—mandatory, I might add—on the standards in reading and writing, science, and social studies. This was a summer school to increase reading, writing, and math all within forty part-time days. We had to accomplish what the regular classroom teachers could not do or at least expand upon a student's repertoire of skills. I took my role as an educational leader seriously. I examined the New York State Standards in English Language Arts thoroughly and expected my teachers to incorporate activities into their lessons. Units on summer activities like insects, the life of ponds, or growing plants were incorporated into reading and writing within the curriculum. The teachers were wonderful, and their expertise was demonstrated on a daily basis.

Over the course of the summer, I learned much about the relaxed atmosphere of summer school. I wanted the teachers to keep their expectations high. These remedial students could shine more than ever because they were not threatened by their overzealous, verbose, please-the-teacher kinds of peers. They became curious. This was something I personally wanted to instill in them. They read to me, and I to them, classroom after classroom, throughout the school. I'd walk around each morning and ask lots of questions, and the students would answer me with newfound language skills, based on what they had just learned. In spite of the summer heat, the lack of materials, the absence of a secretary because we have no money program, and the feeling that we were intruders in someone else's schools, we accomplished much more for the confidence of the children.

Part of the population of the summer school students present in the school attended to learn English as a second language. Some of these children had just arrived to our community from Estonia, Russia, Serbia, Korea, Japan, and other countries. We had children whose parents left their native country because they could not live with a neighboring community. In their child's summer school class, they found that those same ethnic differences were celebrated here, not feared. I took pride in telling people I was the principal of the most ethnically diverse school in all America.

The introduction of food in any institution changes the function of the social group. The first year of summer school, we had all the students in the breakfast room at once. I had student helpers, teaching assistants, and some students help distribute the food. When the students had finished, they were often presented with a ten-minute "window of opportunity" to entertain themselves while they waited for their teacher to take them to class. As the noise increased each morning and students could not hear their teachers call their name, I decided to teach them the camp songs I had learned as a child. I knew that even for the students who did not speak the language, most could easily pick up my simple melodies and could gradually learn the words as we sang them each morning. I also knew that for our nonreaders or low-level readers, I could tie word and song together and increase their literacy as well. So I wrote the words of the songs on a big poster paper: "Row, Row, Row," "Grey Squirrel," "This Little Light of Mine," (we did two—and three part rounds) and many songs with hand motions like "My Hat It Has Three Corners" or "Bingo" (sign language). Good old singing in the summertime. Luckily, I had some teaching assistants with better voices. They taught students too. A song a day is what the students learned. One mother came in and taught a Japanese song. We had gospel. We sang just about all the songs sequentially, as we learned them in order. Each morning after breakfast, we had student "leaders" lead a song, two or three students at a time. It was like a pep rally each morning. Howard Gardner, PhD, would be pleased.

The second year of summer school was easier as a principal. First, we would be housed in one building, with one afternoon program at the school to transition students at the end of the morning. Second, many of the teachers who had been there for academic fun changed their minds about teaching and left the program. I could count on the students spending more of their time reading, writing, and learning basic math and less time having teachers walk students around the building to take up time. We had guest speakers and volunteer readers from the library community program and the senior citizens center. I had planned to have hot lunches, and I actually had a cafeteria helper to provide this to the students. As a result, we could better nourish their hearts and their souls. I paid a youth employment worker out of my own pocket each week to serve as the school secretary, a former student with dyslexia of mine and, as a result of the needed phone-message-taking duties, even her spelling improved over forty days!

The children attended more days of summer school consecutively than in previous years because they were expected to be there and they were engaged from the start of the day. If they did not attend that day, I drove over to their house or apartment to find out why they did not attend. The reading, writing, and math instruction required that the student attend school each day, and believe it or not, most of the children wanted to be there as they had nothing better to do. We had evolved into a believable entity. Parents began to see the summer school as more than just a free child care program and could see the progress in their child's desire to read and write. The best part was when a parent cried in my office because she was so thankful. One student had changed from a disorderly, disinterested child to a student who could not stop reading and writing at home. Many rewards in public education are silently distributed, one child at a time, and I was thankful myself for the parents' enthusiasm. I felt as though I had contributed to our community. During this time, not one administrator came to observe the summer school despite many invitations to stop by and speak with the teachers and the students. It would have been a good reinforcement for the program if one of the eight elementary principals or one of the two middle school principals had dropped by to view our summer school. The super was also invited by myself but showed no interest. Even the director in charge of the summer school only came by to counsel a teacher suspected of using alcohol each morning to get through the day. Even the board of education members who had reluctantly agreed to fund the summer school never appeared. Really. We worked in isolation and without accolades. I decided not to make this an issue but choose to wait until I could write about the lack of interest and support until now.

What was most depressing to me is that I was not evaluated based on the merit of the summer school program, and I had worked hard to make the program work for three years. I figured that my skills had been honed for a more permanent and advanced position in the administrative world. I soon realized that gigs don't beget gigs and that a person is often pegged into a slot by whatever administrative team happens to exist in the moment. The success one achieves in the public school educational life is fleeting and not based on personal achievement. Politics is an essential piece of the administrative team. I don't play politics well. I just do the job the best way I can.

ATTENDANCE

The reported declining standardized test scores and the difficulties meeting the standards in any state in the United Sates has and always has been linked to a child's attendance in school. From the rural farms to the inner-city tenements, those children who participated in the educational system the best were those who came to school well prepared for the rigors of the day. Students came to school whether they had lunch in their lunch pail or bread and jelly in their sacks. They came when they could because they wanted to learn.

Even today, the students who have the toughest time learning how to read, write, learn math, and socialize with their peers stand a better chance of success if they are present! The curriculum may change from one reform to the next, whole language, phonics, Dick and Jane, or Ashanti and Shaniqua, but the key factor is the presence and the attention of the child. This presence is what I call the raw material or (TRM). Children cannot be taught well if they are not present. Fleas, ticks, asthma, colds, lice, scabies, tummy aches, coughs, and the normal childhood diseases like fifths disease, German measles, and flu are all reasons why children do not attend on a daily basis. Immunizations for the chicken pox, measles, and others have helped to cut the rate of absenteeism from school, but children are still missing for more days than they should be out of school compared to other countries.

In terms of attendance, public high schools are nothing more than the playgrounds of what I call the "not fully formed" adults, and we are doing a lousy job as a nation of producing our material given the TRM we are getting each year. The money invested in public schools should be seeking ways to engage our youth in their future or to at least attend school every day. Incentives throughout the country have ranged from cash payment for attendance to links with paid employment. I have no problem with innovative ways to get children to stay in school until a model of civilized behavior can be taught. In today's world, children seem to mature as independent thinkers at a slower pace. They have had a cushier life than their grandparents and are much more influenced by the media. And to this end, we must bear responsibility ourselves for not making children part of the family's daily business, which depends on their chores for our survival. In between soccer practice, music lessons, religious education, arranged play sessions (which just about says it all), homework, practice, Girl Scouts, and church groups, no wonder our children don't have time to vacuum. It is easier to pay an adult under the table to do this work so our children can study. This lack of discipline at home is the root of the undisciplined students in our high schools.

Because there are multiple factors when it comes to attendance, surely 180 days is not too much to ask of students to get up each morning and show up. I have often told my college students that in a few previous generations ago, they would be working on the farms, in the factories, and in their family business. College was for the elite. Women were not even welcome. A few short years ago, and yet, it seems we may be returning to a slower pace of life because of the recession. Maybe children will have fewer material things, more responsibility, and more discipline at home.

In many ways, we have accomplished our goal to increase the number of students in our country with a college diploma, and we should be proud. With such an educated populace compared to many other civilizations around the globe, our diploma paper mill is cranking some pretty impressive numbers. Not enough practical, technical diplomas, but at least students realize now that alternatives, such as the military, still demand a general education diploma. Why then do we, as a nation, spend more time and money in the media on Angelina Jolie / Brad Pitt stories and other "celebratty" idols? What happened to discourse and appreciation of the live arts for entertainment? I had thought that a classical education would bring more support for these endeavors rather than less. The college students today seem to know less about life than more, even as the media explodes with information. Daily attendance in school helps tremendously, but it is only one factor in school engagement.

Students who have parents who change their place of residency every few months in the early school years are at a distinct disadvantage. Consistency is a major dynamic to reinforce daily learning. Changing teachers and methodologies are ever-present examples of disruption of the curriculum. *Huge* gaps in learning are caused by parents who initiate moves in residence during the school year or anytime. The unfortunate children need to switch schools as often as an address changes. Uniformity of instructional technique is disrupted from school to school or district to district. Children do not learn as well when they move from classroom to classroom, school to school. Studies should be conducted to link programs supported by federal funds such as the IDEA, Section 504 regulations, and Title 1 to attendance and movement between schools and districts. I am sure there is a direct relationship to performance in academics and testing. There are enough studies that have been completed showing the relationship between attendance and school performance.

Suspension because of infractions causes more interruption in a student's education, and then, when the student is suspended, the student experiences a lack of instruction by the main teacher and often experiences failure in his/her work. This endless cycle results in another infraction until the student has lost so much time the student has to redo an entire grade. An alternative placement in a different educational setting is often the best way to break the cycle.

We need to rethink the way we educate children today in our 180 daytime school structure. Morris Katz, my grandfather, died of a heart attack as he tried to push his car to get it to start. My father stopped going to school *during the day* at age sixteen to help his mother, Wilma, pay the rent and provide food for himself and his younger brother, Benjamin. My father went to night school in Brooklyn at James Madison High School and completed his high school diploma as he worked in the Macy's stockroom during the day. After serving in the US army in World War II, Sergeant George J. Katz went on to Rutgers University as a result of GI Bill benefit and graduated with a degree in accounting from Rider University in Trenton, New Jersey. He had moved around a lot as a child because his father was a shoe designer and the family had to go where there was work in Ohio, Massachusetts, or New York City. Did this affect his schoolwork?

I am sure. This is what influenced my father to make sure his children stayed put in the same house and schools with as few moves as possible.

The point here is that despite these hardships, school attendance was a family value. Often because my grandmother spoke very little English, George had to register himself and his brother by himself with each move to a new city. The apartments they rented were usually furnished by the landlord, and they all learned to make do with what they had, which was usually nothing. Why can't we develop more night schools, Saturday classes, and even Internet-only high school for those slow morning starters? I'll bet we would increase the number of inner-city high schools who would participate. Give each child a computer/printer/scanner and Skype. Make them sign on by 11:00 AM. I wish this could be part of a plan for an underperforming high school. It would take an adventurous administrator to give it a try.

If more parents would commit to making sure their children attended on a daily basis, children would learn in a consistent manner. It would be a boon to districts to supply assistance to families to help them stay in their home school for the entire year and only make a transition when necessary at the end of a school term. Connecting with a school environment is essential for a student to value their attendance at that school. Administrators who make school inviting and participatory often have better student attendance rates. You can only teach those students who are actually motivated in the classroom and motivated to learn something new.

THE PARENTS

I liked receiving presents from parents when I was working. It meant so much to me to receive a thank-you note, a jar of homemade jelly, or a loaf of banana bread as a thank-you for my work with a parent's child. Small heartfelt tokens meant the parents appreciated my efforts with their progeny. Potted spring flowers, candles, pot holders, and fancy soaps are always appreciated. I heard that the downstate teachers in some regions of my state receive very expensive gifts, and the competition to one-up a teacher has driven many a parent to the mall searching for that perfect gift for the teacher.

The point is not that a gift was necessary from every student I worked with, but it was sometimes the only way I knew I was making a difference. My job was to teach the child, but in more cases than not, I needed to support the parent as well.

This is an aspect of teaching most non-educators do not understand. Especially in the elementary grades, it is important to teach the parents what *we* want their children to learn so the parents can provide practice time or rehearse the skills with their children at home. If you want the children to learn multiplication, the teacher must show the parent the strategies and the language involved and provide the materials if necessary. Do you want the child to read for twenty minutes a night? Ask the parent what they are reading and when they can set up a reading time in their household. Bottom line is, the children who learn anything best, practice, discuss, and play with the materials at home. Homework does not have to be a solitary task. Teachers cannot do this job alone; there just isn't enough time in the school day. Study the behaviors of successful students and you will see extensive parent involvement and effort to provide new experiences and support for the curriculum. Does it take an extraordinary amount of time? Yes.

Now study the children who do not have good parental attention. Those students perform worse at school. The help does not need to come from a parent. This support can come from an older child or any adult. Someone in the household must give the child the time to practice what they have learned during the day. Studies have shown that parental involvement is the key to having the child become a high school graduate in all the United States.

Parents, grandparents, aunties, and caregivers are a crucial piece of the education puzzle. The more the classroom teacher involves the family of the student, the better the student will become a lifelong learner—and that is what we need. To hear about the accomplishments of former students is the ultimate gift you can give a teacher, knowing they had a hand in that child's success. I am most pleased when my former students give me the gift of their time and let me know what they are doing with their life. I have enough soap and candles to last a lifetime.

POWER PERCEIVED

I was offered a position as an interim associate principal at a middle school in my district. After I was contacted by the principal, I went to speak with him and the man who was acting as an interim associate principal, a longtime coworker who had been burned and bruised by the system. He had been serving as an interim for whatever school needed him. He wanted to give me a chance, and I got the position. I owe him a lot for his kindness as I sat with him in a three-day transition period where he taught me the art of referral based middle school discipline. Following the discipline guidelines, considering the infractions, contacting teachers, parents, in-school suspension teachers, etc., were all part of the daily duties. All my previous work in educational theory, curriculum development, and research led me to a police officer type of job in the school.

I found out, after my first day, that the general public of all kinds were often in awe when you revealed that you were a school administrator. In the grocery store, people would immediately recount their own behavioral misdeeds in school and tell you that you had a really hard job. The power adults felt that my new position wielded was amazing to me. In just short of a day, I rose from being a lowly teacher allowed into the halls of the folks who could actually make life-changing decisions, or so I thought.

In practice, my life became pretty mundane. I myself was shocked at the rudeness some of the students and parents displayed and the need for attention all seemed to require. Simple problem-solving skills needed to be taught. Many times, the students would reveal that "he said this, and I said that, and she said this . . . and I'm gonna kick that booty." Frankly, I was amazed at why girls especially had the time to worry about this stuff and why they thought I could help them out of it.

The referrals to the associate principals some teachers wrote for aberrant behavior were ridiculous and should have been handled by the teachers in their classrooms as I had done with my challenging students. The amount of time required to address each one became similar to a factory operation. My father had once told me that if I went to college, I would not have to work in a factory, but here I was, working the discipline diesel engine. Call the student into my office, explain what they did wrong, make a few phone calls, and then send the student to time-out or back to class.

Each day was different though, and when students fought, I would have to use my reporting and lawyer skills to try to sort out who was at fault, why the students responded the way they did, and what consequences would be doled out. I scheduled principal's hearings so the principal could suspend out-of-school offenders. As an associate principal, I attended several superintendent's hearings where the recommendations for disciplinary reasons could exceed ten days of out-of-school suspension. For some students, this is what they ultimately wanted—to be out of school for a period of time. For others, it could be devastating as it interrupted their classes and they would fall further behind, even with the required daily tutoring outside the school grounds. Still, it was not the same as being in the classroom, and this system seemed to reinforce disengagement and increased student apathy.

For the parents of students who made violent decisions, their lives became completely disrupted, and they were often not a happy lot—so much for a college-bound diploma for all. Some folks felt their child could do no wrong. Other parents would make their child sleep in the truck for the night despite the chilly weather. My job was to preach safety in the school at all costs. Children bring a lot of emotional baggage from home into the school each day. Their nights are not filled with Brady Bunch happiness and a caring family. Many children these days are experts at computer games but can't solve interpersonal problems with their peers and aren't learning how to do the ten things they were supposed to learn in kindergarten, like sharing, respect, and turn-taking.

Here is an interesting story. The middle school in which I was an assistant principal was about two miles from a shopping mall down the highway. Sometimes students would leave school and walk to the mall to hang out after they signed in or even before homeroom began—off the bus and then bolt through the neighborhoods to the mall. I became friendly with the manager of the mall, and we developed a ruse to call the students to the mall office saying they had won a prize. For fifteen-year-old girls, anything free from the mall is an instant reward. They would fall for it, and I'd have the mall security guards keep them in the office until their parents came to pick them up and bring them back to school. It worked like a charm. Nothing I had done before in the schools or in my educational administration courses prepared me for a position as a security officer, but that is what it felt like many times that year. Perhaps education administration courses such as "How to Talk to an Angry, Armed Student" or "What to Tell an Upset Parent" should be added to the curriculum. Theory of educational administration is wonderful, but some concrete tactics would have been very helpful. Luckily, I understood child development and the demands of most of today's parents.

My best buddies were the cute young guys in the gray suits, neat purple ties, and out-there hats—the New York State Police. Since our school was outside the city police jurisdiction, these men (no women yet) would stride into our school with confidence and help us in any way they could, including picking up our students hitchhiking on the highway on the way to the mall. They were the first I called for the incident that occurred on my watch one early morning.

I'd get to school first in the morning, would open up the office, and start the day checking my e-mail and the voice mail. At about eight one morning, the phone rang; I answered it in the normal way, and I heard a voice say, "There's a bomb in your building." Then the caller hung up before I could speak. I held the receiver in my hand for about one minute, and I thought *No one is here yet. Did I hear this correctly? What happens if I didn't say anything and we went along our business? Then again, what if it was real?* I sprung into action and informed my secretary, who had just arrived. The piece of paper with the district bomb protocol was nowhere to be found. I called the state police (no 911 in our area yet). My principal had planned to come in late that day. The superintendent wasn't in yet. The assistant superintendent had just arrived in her district office. Time was ticking (no pun intended). I called transportation and told them to keep the kids on the buses and we could do this because our school was the final run of the morning. I made an announcement for all the faculty and staff to meet in the front hallway. Students who walked to school or who were driven by parents started arriving, and we kept the doors locked and the children outside of the building, far away from the front doors. I asked some teachers to keep the students calm and to tell them that we had to keep them out of the building until the fire department came. It began to rain. Fire, police, rain, bomb-sniffing dogs, sirens, (now) principal, and assistant superintendent were the only images that flashed in front of me. This was the state of the educational system on this day, but all too often, throughout the public schools in the United States . . .

We caught the student who made the bomb phone call within a day just as I had suspected. He told a friend about it, and the friend was sent to tell me. Students always talk. It is just a matter of time before we found out who did it. I knew the student. He had been in my office before because he had been picked on by a group of students. He was an annoying kid and not as innocent as he looked. He never came back to school. He completed middle school and high school at a private school out of state.

I received a nice letter from the assistant superintendent thanking me for the way I had handled the situation. The next year, the superintendent gave my job to the woman she wanted to have the position the year before, as though my performance had not mattered or existed. The new hire was from out of town, and I spent four days training her to do the job. At the end of my training, the new hire remarked, "I think you did a great job, and I don't know why you weren't hired for the position permanently."

I went back to my old position as a support teacher at an elementary school, kind of like an assistant principal without the title or pay. My year as an assistant principal in the middle school was the year I learned about discipline and why adolescents' brains are not fully formed.

In the words of Ghandi, "They cannot take away our self-respect if we do not give it to them."

HOW DO YOU JUDGE
A LEADER?

I played by the district rules for eight years in this centrally isolated small city school district in Upstate New York before I started to think out of the box. I had been a Girl Scout for my entire school career, including high school, and as a result, I had an understanding of how to earn the right to advance in a career. I thought making it to the top was like working on various badges in Girl Scouting. If you earned enough "badges," you would naturally progress. I knew how to earn first class and get to the top of a hierarchy within an institution. If you do everything correctly, you too can rise above and be a leader. Right? Anyway, wasn't the principal the smartest member of the school? So how hard could it be? If I worked hard, I could be a principal, super, or whatever.

I was smart and ambitious and also quite naive. I did not think politics, old-girl networks and personality preferences could get in the way of success. The glass ceiling was in place in this school district, but I didn't get to that room in the house yet, so I would keep viewing the house with optimism for a while. As I progressed in my career, I began to I feel as though I was always on the outside looking into the "room." I could not get past the whims of the super, no matter how much I worked, campaigned, volunteered, or whatever. My "leader" was determined to keep me in my place or send me away to a different district. I refused to leave. I lived in this community and was determined to make a difference here with these kids.

After a while, I began to realize that people in educational leadership positions were not smarter than I, but these people knew more about certain elements of the "game," such as school politics, networking, and trust in friends so you would not be screwed behind your back.

And so I began to wonder, *What did the administrators of this school district know that I didn't, and how could I obtain that knowledge?* I never wanted to be a principal at that point. I liked having summers off. I had a young family. But I was tired of being led by people who hadn't read a book for centuries. These were the good old boys. They were the men who had majored in some sport at some state college. Jeez. This couldn't be rocket science. Nothing could be harder than my master's degree, my high school honors classes, or my lab science courses in college.

By this time in my career, I already had a number of different educational leaders i.e., principals in various schools and in various districts during the course of my career. All of them had their likes and dislikes, habits and curiosities.

One principal cleaned the tables every day at lunch so he would get to know the children. He took me on a home visit one day in his car so I could see just how the people in poverty lived. I learned never to get out of a car if the dog was in the yard and not chained up during these visits.

Another principal, Sister George Mary, would round me up at the Catholic school and sit me down for a little chat in her office with a huge picture of Jesus Christ looming over her chair.

"Oh, I heard you are dating a Catholic boy," she said one day early in the school year.

"Yes," I said meekly. In the back of my mind, I was thinking, *Yes, I was dating a Catholic, but he hated established religion of any kind, and he was not a boy, but a man—and whose business is this anyway?*

"Well, if there is anything I can do to help . . ." she offered.

"Thank you," I said politely.

Meanwhile, I was the token Jew in the entire school. Was she curious, or did she get points for conversions? Anyway, this nun ran the school with an iron hand, and the result was the quietist, most civilized school I had worked in during my thirty-three years in public education. I tried to learn what she did, and basically, I concluded that God was on her side so she could use sin, the parent, and expulsion in her discipline tool belt under her robes.

Once I had a principal who told me never to speak in administrative meetings because then the team would know my agenda. I understood that this woman was different, but paranoia was not a characteristic I thought was necessary for a good leader. It seemed she believed that no one should ever really know your basic opinions because they could be used against you in the future. So meeting after meeting during the year, I watched her say nothing during administrative team sessions, nod her head, and drift off.

I once asked a principal how he handled the pressure of managing two schools at once. The district administrators couldn't seem to find an interim to handle one of the schools, and this principal had volunteered to do both positions. I was completing my internship in educational administration and was exhausted working in just one school. As we walked up the steps of his school together, he said, "You have to pace yourself." Good words of advice. I use them even today. This man died of a heart attack while on vacation about three months after our conversation. I guess everyone's pace is different.

There was one principal who had a terrible lateral lisp. So much for the idea of principal being the perfect specimen of humanity. Since I was the speech therapist in the building at the time, I gave him my schedule and told him I was blocking out a time once a week for him to come in to see me. I couldn't stand another "pledge of allegiance" with that lisp in all the S sounds. He never did come and see me, and he laughed it off each time I mentioned it. Fine. Speak that way the rest of your life.

The straw that broke the camel's back, and convinced me I needed more education myself, was when I was in one school as a support teacher (like an assistant principal, but in the teachers' union) and someone told me that I could be liable if something happened and I was in charge of the building without administrative certification. Since my current principal had gout and an enormous penchant for fishing, I was left alone in charge of the building for many days. No phone call ahead of time from him. I would find out I was in charge of the school when I walked in the door each morning. I realized that on any given day, I was the adult decision maker for the entire elementary school of more than four hundred students and a combined staff of about eighty people. It was I and the underpaid school secretary who were responsible for the daily operation. On one of the final days this scenario occurred, I made a decision to enroll in the local educational administration program for a post-master's degree certificate in school district administration (SDA) at State University of New York at Cortland. After all the principals I had worked for, what inspired me to finally sign up for additional coursework in education administration was curiosity (what did those ex-jock principals know that I didn't know?) and an overall fear of being sued for being responsible for a building without the proper certification and approval by the board of education.

I began the coursework in educational administration for other reasons too. The first reason was to learn what factors differentiated a school leader from the regular ordinary teachers. The second reason was to learn something new I might use later on in life and, by doing so, enhance my own basic salary. According to our teacher's contract, I was able to get a small stipend added to my base salary for each of the nine credits I completed. The third reason was to allow myself some time when no one, including my own children, could ask me to do something they could do themselves. I needed a break once a week for three hours from any children, but I wanted it to be productive time. Since I needed to do something each week for myself, I looked at the three-hour classes after work as a yoga class or a night out with the girls instead. I would be assuring other opportunities for financial gain for my family in the future. I managed to obtain inexpensive tuition waivers from a teacher who had no need for them, and I began three years of courses one at a time—fall, spring, and the first summer session—at the college that was a thirty-minute drive from my house. When I completed the coursework, I managed to obtain a full-year paid internship (from hell) in a school at a rural elementary school with a mentor principal less able than I was to deal with the trials and tribulations of running a public school. The internship experience is an entirely different essay.

As part of the education administration program, I decided that I should concentrate on learning how to effectively change adult teachers' educational practices without causing them to become fearful and threatened. Many of the papers I wrote for different classes dealt with teacher/adult change, and I developed an extensive bibliography, working each paper around the specific topic of different classes rather than inventing the wheel each time and picking a variety of topics.

The classes in the program themselves were a piece of cake, especially after a science-based master's degree like the one I finished in speech pathology. They were geared toward the full-time working person during the day, taking classes in the evening—the older kind of student. During the three years I matriculated at SUNY Cortland, I had signed up for three courses taught by the same professor whom I thought was the most honest, the most knowledgeable about the field, and the most humorous. After the first semester I had him as a professor, he told me I was a decent writer and should write about my experiences. He said he always anticipated reading my papers with glee! With his encouragement, I began writing short essays about my experiences in the public school system so I would not forget the details. These essays became the precursor to this book.

Writing about the events in the district became my form of therapy. No one could criticize my thoughts, and I would not have to play nice to anyone as long as freedom of speech existed in this country. I would write without using real names and not identify the district by name. My goal was to expose the waste of money in the public schools, the stupid politics that occurs on a daily basis, and several factors that might contribute to a struggling student's success and to document my frustrations as I tried to find positions of leadership within the district. I also wanted a forum for my thoughts and others like mine to discuss why public education is a great concept but still needs much improvement. Writing essays of frustration with the current system in my own district would become part of my quest to evolve into the perfect school leader so I could make a difference in young people's lives and share what I have learned with others.

CHA-CHA CHAIN, CHAIN OF FOOLS

One would think that after a while, the chain of command in the public school system would be filled with the enlightened. (Cue the music.) I had thought those figureheads knew everything there was to know about educating children. I had thought that public school leaders read every weekend about the newest trends and research in the field. Wrong. Total mythology. Yes, some do read articles in trade papers about education but most try to do nothing related on their off time, which is not that much anyway due to the district's demands. How, in God's name, could a person in administration have the time to read on what's happening if most of the free time from the job is spent hanging with folks who are *not* in the field of education?

Take many public school superintendents. They golf, they ski, and they play tennis. They have boats. They watch football, hockey, soccer, and basketball. Pray tell then *when* do they have time to read, reflect, and review what they are doing? OK, in the car driving/flying from one convention to the next is when they may have some time to read, but not likely.

But really, any surprise that they then pick people most like themselves to work with them? Any brilliant ideas out there about *who* gets the primo jobs? How about the person most like the superintendent and their board? Try for divergent thinkers? Nah, too different. Try to incorporate those leaders with great teaching experience? Nah, they have been in the field too long. How about the folks that truly love children? Nope. Mmmm. Too soft. How about the school leaders who have presented and published at conventions and trade papers? Yikes, too driven. What about those education leaders who try to include reforms based on scientific research? Hmmm, could be too radical and cause waves. Good thing Steve Jobs surrounded himself with people who had opposite character traits from himself, or nothing would have come out of his love for different printing fonts.

How does a super end up picking her buddies to lead a school district? Superintendents pick those people for leadership positions whom they themselves can hang out with and have something in common with like discussing the latest Rotary stuff, golf club clinics, and boating tips. In my experience, supers are not interested in hanging out and working with a young yahoo teacher who wants to become a school leader and change education practice unless you are really cute and have some really attractive ideas. This is sad but still true. Trying to introduce a new reading program takes reams of paper and tons of e-mails to convince even one board member or one principal if he/she has no background in reading development and sees no reason for the change. It's all about the money and how it is spent. Teacher-initiated change in direction is so often needed and so valuable, but it can become too much effort. As a result, the teachers continue status quo even when not effective for a portion of the population, and the young wannabe administrator starts to lose her/his mojo because she/he does not hang in the same places or have the same outside interests.

I once had a superintendent who told me he could not hire me as a middle school principal, saying, "I already got one woman up there at the high school and one woman down there at the elementary school. If I hire you, by God, the whole district would be run by women. Board ain't gonna take a liking to that!" What a stupid, stupid man. I would not want to work for him anyway, so I said, "Thank you for your time," and walked out. I secretly prayed that the women there would drive him crazy and out of his job by way of heart attack or stroke. I could have sued him for his remarks . . .

Occasionally, the young upstart will be hired by a super for amusement (like a cat toy) at some lower-level job and still may be part of the administrative team. This would go on for a few years for the entertainment of the super or to complete gofer-type activities. The person hired would have no clue, but those around him/her would be laughing our silly "you know what" behind his/her back as he/she walked down the hallway in the board office. "There goes the toy," we would say.

Anyway, a super can always farm out his work and hire consultants. Part of the super's job these days is to be able to pick the correct consultant for a few months for the district. A consultant would be hired for communication, as well as one for special education and another for systems analysis. How about hiring a consultant for a change in superintendent? Hiring a consultant means the district administrators don't have to do the research themselves for a recommendation to the board and don't have to keep the person on staff forever. I have yet to see effective results from an outside consultant hired by the district for *any* topic so far. It seems like a huge waste of money. How about asking the members of "The Public School Island" for input and whom to kick off the island? Don't think for a minute that all of what I am saying is untrue. What I write here will be unpopular, but everything is true throughout the public school districts in New York State.

The chain of command is often built of steel and with a few links that have come from the unknown outside circle. It may appear that a search for a position goes on (nationwide, of course). In the end, the person hired often knew someone who knew the other person who was related to the brother-in-law of the board member and on and on. Funny how after a nationwide search, the administrator hired lives only forty-five minutes away and has been acting as a councilman, alderman, shoe designer, and gifts consultant but started a career in education and wants back in again. "They bring a breath of experience."

So the chain remains unbroken, and the length has increased to include members of the same representative group of folks all thinking alike. Isn't that nice? Isn't that tidy? Think of it as control of the group. The super gets to pick all his/her homey friends and then leave for another opportunity. This happens all the time.

Isn't *that* why public education doesn't represent the views of a wider constituency? For most of the boards of education in New York State, the stakeholders do not represent all the pockets of various groups within the schools. There may be some representation, but when you actually watch, their participation is often drowned out by a more formally educated vocal member. Ask how many board members have had their own kids suspended. For true change in the right direction, you need a board of education that looks like the kids in the district. Our own board has so many professors from the local Ivy League education university that it is no wonder why they just don't get the poor minority kid in the school and what he needs to survive each day. And you guys voted not to have high school summer school but just funded another administrative position to crunch numbers? Are you supposed to be able to do that yourself?

I challenge the boards of education all over the country to begin hiring men and women as superintendents and administrators who have a direct interest in the community and who are living within the community in which they work, not forty-five minutes away. I challenge them because the only way to really know what is needed for children to succeed is a sense of what is happening in their daily lives. When administrators live in a different town forty-five minutes away, I have to question their loyalty. Besides, there is nothing wrong with a "grow and support your own" concept. Oftentimes, these hires are the ones who stay for the long term because they live and participate within the same community. They have a vested interest. Please don't hire someone from out of your state when there are pools of candidates who have lived next door to you and worked with your kids. Hiring not from within the community just reinforces all the inappropriate drama in public schools already.

EDUCATION WEIGHS IN . . .

In educational administration, there are many human "desource" practices, which do not make any sense for the growth and stability of a public school district. A person has a better chance of being hired as an administrator if he/she teaches for a short time (not too much), goes away to work in a small district or another state, and then comes back to the original district. The experience gained somewhere else is often thought of as more valuable, more significant than if the person had remained in the same district but had taught effectively, volunteered for committees, and/or had developed with families over time. I don't know why this is true, but it is a custom in many public school districts. The idea of supporting or "growing your own" administrator exists in a few places, often rural areas where no one else would live unless they have family in the area or a significant reason to stay. By the way, an affirmative action affirms the action you want to take. That is the real working definition of the law in my district. We hire by race all the time, but *shush*, don't tell anyone, and I hope the public school officers don't read the essays this far and find out what I wrote, but it is true. Is it a dirty little secret? Yes.

All the regular staff's treatment in a public school is often a disgrace. Remember that the administrators making decisions about personnel are generally folks trained in the teaching of some subject like physical education but are not trained in human resources or counseling. Staff or teacher, administrator or custodian, humans in public education are often treated very poorly in the public school workplace by the school administration and even the board of education. It is an equal-opportunity, poorly managed system in even the best districts in the country. Managed by educators who have never taken a course in business or communications, textbook mistakes in the hiring, firing, and reassignment of duties are commonplace. Often, not a thought is given to first communicate changes to employees personally but rather through the grapevine or word of mouth. I shudder to think how technology may even have made things worse. Confidentiality is a joke.

Here are some wonderful true-to-life stories to show how people are more valuable when they leave a district and other types of hiring practices that happened to real people employed as administrators in a public school:

A woman I'll call Mary worked in the school district as a teacher of consumer science in a middle school. She left the small, isolated, centrally located school district in Upstate New York, went to live in another state for a few years, and acquired certification as an administrator in that state. In her previous school district, she was not very highly regarded but rather as someone who had done a mediocre job in her former positions, but now that she had gone away and worked in another public school in another state, she became a more viable and valuable candidate for a directorship. Never mind that there were highly qualified people internally in the community who could have done a better job in the new position. This didn't matter. "Brunhilde" or Mary went away. Her experience was worth more now, and she was hired for an administration position despite her previous below-average demonstration of pedagogy.

In the world of competitive sports, players who work hard and perform well are often rewarded with positions on elite teams that make a lot of money. In the world of public school education, politics plays such an important role in obtaining jobs. This concept is a little known dirty secret. Just like in sports, deals are made between "players," and people are traded from one "team" or district to another.

A human resource officer I once knew worked in a district for about ten years and was handpicked by the super. He made life difficult for many employees from various unions such as the teachers' union and the employees'/staff unions within the district. Always on the lookout to catch some kind of employee mistake, he himself became a "trade" when he outlived his usefulness and grew out of favor with a change in the board of education members. The old adage "He who laughs last laughs best" could be applied to this man because, after his trade, he was not granted tenure in the new district, and like many of the former employees of his original district, he was ditched and out on the street looking for a job. By the way, this human resource director had never attended a public school in his life; his entire education had taken place in private religious schools, including his college education. He had only taught for a short time but was hired because the super at the time felt he could best be manipulated by the super to do her dirty work, which he did well up to a point. When he was originally hired, the super was the only one who wanted him.

When Mayor Bloomberg of New York City was elected and took office, he decided to reorganize the New York City public school system. Mayor Bloomberg appointed a man named Joel Stein to the position of commissioner of education for the New York City public schools. Mr. Stein had a background in law and had never been a teacher in a public school. He had never been a public school administrator. Despite his lack of formal experience, Mr. Stein cooked up the correct recipe for public school success based on his own public school experience and the advice of his advisors. He shook up the bag, tossed out the brown lettuce, and created a new salad for each borough with new literacy programs for all students. This process ruffled feathers, and many people in educational administration who had been comfortable with their positions directing continually failing schools were shocked, stressed, and fired or given an incentive to retire. Articles were written in the New York City newspapers and national magazines such as *Time* about the new mandated curriculum. Teachers' unions and administration unions went crazy to no avail. Mr. Stein continued his campaign with the maximum support from Mayor Bloomberg. If a school does not perform, you throw out the administrators, right? This is just like the developing nations who change their leaders whenever change is needed or wanted.

If you change the old-guard administrators and put into place new educational leaders, with little or no experience and few additional resources, will this really change the way students perform? This is a dissertation question far beyond the reaches of this book and could be debated for years to come.

Within the concept of the instructional leadership lies the model that there are the workers who drive the instruction (administrators) and those that actually deliver the instruction (teachers). If the administrators know little about the normal development of children and the standards for literacy established by their own state, it is difficult for them to assess the competency of the teachers. Also, the needs of the consumers (students) can be vastly different from one public school from another. Time and time again had I witnessed administrators hired for various positions without the certification necessary from even my own state of New York. Therefore, their knowledge of educational state standards was limited, and they had difficulty appraising the effectiveness of the teachers and the curriculum.

It takes a skilled educator to learn the needs and learning styles of students and to be able to adjust the curriculum and teach according to the breadth of strengths and weaknesses within one class session. The administrators with little background of the state standards are the *least* likely to be able to direct the school districts with regard to educational reform since they are often the farthest from the product (the literate student as the consumer). When a new administrator takes a position in a public school he may find the learning curve to be quite steep, and it may take up to five years for him to truly understand the population.

Of course, it takes about this amount of time to uncover the weaknesses of the administrator before he/she moves on to a different position in another state. The relentless revolving door of administration is such a detriment to a community, but it is the only way a person can advance to a higher and more lucrative position in education administration. So change is continual, and the pupils and teachers can become the vehicles for the administrator to enhance his/her career. This sounds like a pessimistic point of view, but it is reality and another function of the system that is never revealed to the public. If an administrator stays in a position for more than five years, there must be external reasons, such as family nearby, in order for that person to be satisfied, or they are not so ambitious. In our public school district, it is not uncommon for a school to have experienced nine different administrators over the course of fifteen years. Sad but true.

As a result of the unremitting flux in the administration in our schools, certain major problems in education are never really addressed. An example of this is when our system fails students over and over again and the core problems are not changed. Our student failure in the high school graduation rate across the country is just one statistic. The administrators have themselves failed to figure out how to keep all students engaged within the system for four years. "Duh," as my students would say.

Since our country's global economy is tied into the economy of many other nations, it is imperative that our American students become literate not only in English but also in many different languages. This will require a reevaluation of curriculum for all students, which is not even in the thoughts of most administrators. Also, because choices are so limited for American students and the length of their required participation is so long—eighteen years old (completion of the twelfth grade is the norm)—the fact that the dropout rate is so high should come as no surprise to anyone. Children are developing at a faster rate and yet are slower to assume responsibility of the adulthood responsibilities in our communities. We have a system so archaic and nonfunctional that even the most avant-garde administrators fail to realize a massive overall is needed. When 50 percent of the country's 17 year olds are not in some kind of program, all of society suffers. How can administrators ever get to the solution when they are jumping from job to job every few years?

POLITICS AND PLAYGROUNDS—STILL ABOUT HIRING

There really needs to be a required undergraduate course in the teaching education curriculum called How to Play in the Sandbox. This is not about creating curricula relevant to the age group. The course syllabus will not cover the types of Piagetian premath activities that one can create for a classroom. The class will simply learn how to maneuver around and about the hierarchies of reaching the top position in educational administration, whatever you aspire to be—principal, director, assistant superintendent, district superintendent, and so forth.

In this proposed course, one learns how to play politics to get the position you want when you want it.

For years, I have read biographies of famous leaders and books about being the one-minute manager, how to run a company, or what you need to do to be successful. I still need to keep reading because I haven't always been one of the chosen who gets the job. It hurts. What they say is that the job wasn't a fit. Baloney. Bottom line is, somebody knows how to do this better than I do? You know, schmooze all the time. (Why read this book then, huh?) After all, if she (I, the author) couldn't obtain her desired position, what makes you think she should write a book about educational administration?

Rejection. It is part of the journey in education, in business, in life. I have had so many rejection letters for administration positions I know I could wallpaper my bathroom with, or maybe two bathrooms. This is a joke in my house. I thought I was the only one in the world with so many ding letters until I met a woman, a high school associate principal, who told me she had so many letters of rejection you could do her house in letters. She said she was keeping them all (I throw mine out now) and was going to publish them in a book. I asked her if I could reference her book in mine so folks could get a chance to see them, and she said that I could. Someday.

Experience does not always count. At least, I value experience. What some may call experience translates rapidly to others as an entire list of other descriptors such as hardened, opinionated, rigid, difficult to work with, questionable allegiance, old fashioned, and on and on. Not descriptors of me or my style of course, just other people I have known. *In other words, younger people will be hired over those with years of teaching so they can be molded by central office to match the whims and desires of the school district.* Older teachers with great credentials need not apply. It is too much trouble. It is too much work to get them to see the ways of the chosen young leaders. What a waste of money. Here we have trained lots of people who live in our town. We have invested in and grown them, but they are not going to work with us (or do what we want).

I obviously need to learn the art of schmooze and politics. I suppose that the lessons I learned in the sandbox, like sharing and turn-taking, are not those that lead to the money-paying jobs. It seems that in the district I know best, throwing sand in someone's face and snatching the shovel works best. After all, who's looking?

CLIMBING THE ROCK WALL

The words "You are never a prophet in your own land" still baffles me in the educational world. The belief is simple. As I have already written, to improve your skills, you must leave the institution you are working for, go to another institution to make mistakes, and steal their ideas. Then you can come back to lead the original district you left. Why is this acceptable as a matter of course? Or you can do an internship in educational administration, but *don't think you will be hired here permanently*. This seemed to be the current philosophy of one of the superintendents of our district, who seemed to be outstaying her welcome. After all, she had to move to come here, so nah, nah, nah, nah. You will need to move too. OK, let me explain this in detail. You get a job teaching in your discipline, whether it is social studies, special education, or physical education. You are a good teacher. You present papers at state and national conventions even without district financial support. You go the extra mile with parents and kids, and they all respect and love you. You do all the right things like providing extra help after school, volunteering to chaperone dances, providing transportation in your own car so disadvantaged youth can attend events, and giving out your personal phone number so you can be reached at all times. You apply for a position in the district and, *zing*, another person with no experience at that level (elementary, middle, whatever), from a different state, gets the job. OK, that was a quirk, and you begin to realize you must hone your leadership skills.

You participate in district committees and actually attend *all* the meetings. You lead committee work, serve as a summer school administrator, and work every weekend without extra pay to make sure the program is excellent. You apply for another district job. *Whoosh*, a person with no experience at the building level, no ties to the community, a few years of teaching in a private Catholic school, and currently working for the state department gets the job.

As a result, you begin to search for answers as to why you did not get an interview or the job. There usually is no reason they can give because if the committee did tell you, then it would probably be an illegal reason like you aren't of the correct minority background, or you have too many hidden agenda tied to the community, or you won't work because your skills don't match our needs (that is a nice response). In any case, you will never find out, and don't think you shouldn't take it personally because you should.

It is like climbing the rock wall at our local university. At first, there are people to guide you, encourage you, and hold onto you if you fall. The wall contains nooks and crannies to hold onto, and the edifice ascends about three stories. If you make it to the top without falling, you have accomplished something and can then try to climb a real mountain without help. Applying and getting positions in educational administration is like the rock wall. There are lots of people to encourage you in the beginning. When you reach the top, however, you are on your own. Those who ask for assistance are weak. Those who seek to stay within the confines of their own district that trained them have not experienced a real mountain and will not have the respect of the administrators who have climbed another wall. At least this is how it is perceived in this little, tiny, centrally isolated Mecca in the middle of New York State.

The amazing thing is that a district will spend tons of money to train you, but look elsewhere for its hires. Not all school districts. Many will prefer their own to hiring outsiders so that the learning curve is not as steep and the recognition that ties to the community will be beneficial to the youth involved.

However, this district that I worked in seems to value the complete opposite thinking. It seemed that if you hired from the outside, more would be contributed as if you could increase test scores by filling a position with someone from another state.

Time after time, this district would advertise and conduct huge searches for administrator positions. Time after time, the people would come, stay three years, and then split. Then the process would begin again. As a consumer and taxpayer, I know that this process costs quite a bit of money. One advertisement for one day in the Sunday *New York Times* can cost thousands of dollars, not to mention ads in the trade papers such as the *Chronicle of Higher Education* and the local papers.

Since each person is chosen by committee and each union must (or is supposed to) send at least one or two representatives to the committee, then substitutes must be paid to cover the teacher, and productive time is lost for every individual. The next time a budget is presented by your local school district, try to find the itemized costs of recruitment. Chances are, those expenses are hidden within the super's budget or buried under another line, such as human resources. The costs can be exorbitant and wastes precious money that should be used directly for the children. Some districts provide transportation to and from the district, hotel, and even meals with other district employees and the candidate so they help choose the "best" applicant.

Hiring from within is so much cheaper, and if all the taxpayers knew about these hidden public education costs, most would be outraged. Budgets would not pass, and music and art and sports would be cut. It will take a person with *real* guts at the top of the food chain to stop these practices. As a taxpayer myself, I cringe when I hear the district is entertaining potential contenders from Florida, Virginia, etc., and paying all their expenses to come here for three days or more.

Some supers are taking advantage of some programs like the educational administration program at Columbia University in New York City. In this case, the grow-your-own philosophy allows supers to pick leaders within their public school community and take classes over the summer, and eventually, they will be assigned a position within the district. This also means somebody currently in a principal's position will probably be given the boot to make room for the hand-selected, trained person. This is a new approach, and time will tell if the folks trained by our district will stay in our district and acquire certification (and another piece of paper as well) from Columbia University, paid for by state taxes and other people's money.

As I have stated before, supporting and encouraging employees to advance from within is so much better for so many reasons. Most supers who have confidence in their own staff and their own abilities recognize this early on; those that do not seem to enjoy the game of recruit, hire, dismiss, recruit, hire, and dismiss every year. Kind of like buying a new pair of shoes, except it isn't about shoes; it is about children and a literate society in the future and somebody else's moola.

Sometimes the swinging door swings so much and so hard even tenured human resource directors who have promoted these practices in the past get hit from behind and slide down the rock wall themselves!

HUMBLE IS AS HUMBLE DOES

Sometimes I have to eat my words and say that I have been grateful for so many opportunities within our public school district. But just as climbing the wall, I had to be careful to make sure someone was beneath me holding the rope as I climbed. I took advantage of every opportunity in the area of leadership in the district that provided a higher paycheck I could use for the benefit of my family.

When I returned from a trip to the Netherlands with my husband one August, I received a phone call from a middle school principal informing me that I was the second preferred candidate for the position of associate principal. I was not surprised. After all, I had been interviewed while I had a dislocated knee and I was on crutches. I was in a wheelchair (after being principal in the summer school without difficulty) for most of the time. I guess I had a picture of me racing down the hallway in my chair chasing students into classrooms, and the committee couldn't quite grasp this picture. I knew my disability would be temporary, but they didn't.

One whole hour went by, and I received another phone call that day from the high school principal. He asked me to come in for an interview for an interim position as an associate principal. He had managed to secure extra funds for that year from the central office for an additional position, and my name was traded. I informed him about my condition, and he didn't seem to think it would be a problem. I figured I would go and help fill up their candidate pool, and that would be that.

When I crutched into the office, I was told to sit in a small conference room. There I would speak with three people—three associate principals, one on his way out of the job to be a principal in New York City. I answered their questions for about one hour and found my way out. While I was leaving, I saw two of my colleagues walk in to do the same kind of interview. I figured that they were laughing so hard at seeing me interviewed for a discipline job on crutches—that they felt they had it in the bag.

I was called by the principal the very next day, and he offered me the job.

HIGH SCHOOL MAVEN

When I received a phone call that afternoon telling me I had the position if I wanted it, I couldn't believe it. I was on crutches and in a wheelchair for at least six more weeks. I guess they were desperate. So I started as an assistant principal in a one-thousand-six-hundred-pupil high school. I had the responsibility of discipline for eight hundred students whose last names fell between *A* and *L*. I hope the board of education is reading this right now. I also had teacher supervisory duties for the science and math departments, social studies, and physical education. I oversaw the in-school suspension room, was the parent-teacher association (or the PTA) administrative representative, and had to learn a new computer program to track everything. I would not need two good legs. I'd need a cape, a magic sword, and some higher powers. This was to be a one-year position and may/may not be renewed.

Within the first week, I acquired an office, a secretary, and a whole bunch of problems with a relatively dysfunctional team consisting of a social worker, a psychologist, a guidance counselor, and several department chairs who were not talking to one another. Dream job! I held these ghastly weekly meetings, developing an agenda sometimes four minutes before the meetings. These folks all talked about one another behind their backs and were minimally effective when it came to dealing with difficult students.

Something had to change. I told them that they each had to take their own notes during meetings, that I wasn't going to do it, and that someone else, rotating, would be in charge of the agenda. We would meet for one period a week—that's it. Above all else, our discussions would be child-centered, not adult-centered, with action steps for each professional to be completed by the next week.

There are many stories to tell during that year as an assistant principal in the high school. Overall, I saw children who were not engaged in the school for a variety of reasons. Some students came to school for the socialization aspects, and these students spent most of their time in the cafeteria during all the lunch periods. I would go to the cafeteria and urge, cajole, and threaten them to go to class, and they still wouldn't go unless I had them escorted by the security guards. They were holding court in the cafeteria, and who was I to interrupt their social time? These students didn't want to work in school—just hang out in school.

There were fights. There were fights between girl groups and guy groups. There were fights between the rural kids and the city kids. How does this fit into achieving New York State standards? Well, if you are suspended from school for fighting, you get behind in your classes, you get poorer grades, and you lack the information necessary to pass the regents to gain the only diploma offered now in New York State. One fight can change your life. And the fighting was often for stupid reasons like "I didn't like the kid's face" or "She looked at me." Try to rationalize this to a sixteen-year-old.

In fact, my own children were worried about little five-foot me in that environment. I wasn't at all afraid, I told them. I have a radio, security guards at my beck and call, and kids who do like me. I never worried about my own safety.

What did concern me was the lack of respect these children had for themselves and for one another. Public high school can be the most difficult places to navigate for a student these days. In our one-thousand-six-hundred-student high school, the students self-sorted into groups, identifying themselves with a certain type of uniform, just as they did when I was in high school. In my high school days, there were the female preppies who wore wool skirts and Weejun loafers. In today's high schools, female preppies wear brand names such as Hilfiger and Gap. There were the female hoods in my day who wore black skirts, black stockings, and white sneakers. Today the female hoods wear tight jeans and tight tops and show off their belly buttons and the tops of their boobies. We could do an entire sociological study of groups and their own choice of dress in American high schools over the course of the last one hundred years.

No matter what group the students came from, some were just plain disrespectful. Even when you hold a principal's hearing with the student and the guardian present, the student can display some attitude. In most cases, I understood this posturing to be the results of insecurity, lack of confidence, and just plain being scared. Children always respond to kind words and interest in their own endeavors. That doesn't mean that they can be trusted to tell the truth, can interpret the truth, or are in the habit of telling the truth. Some students are hard to read and have tough shells to crack. These were the students I enjoyed working with the most. If you can figure out their motivation, you can usually win them over.

The worst part about the position was chaperoning the dances. At first, I actually looked forward to these events when I first began until one night. It was a spring dance. There were two associate principals and one assistant principal on that night with about six parent chaperones and a security guard in a golf cart covering the parking lot for extra cash.

We had an established protocol for checking students into the dance. I was one of the two APs at the door. If the students left, they were not allowed to return. The students all looked wonderful, especially the girls with their flowing dresses, their beautifully coiffed hair, and their perfume lingering as they entered the dance. I remember thinking how lovely this evening would be. Then about forty-five minutes into the dance, all hell broke loose.

I was summoned into the girls' bathroom by an anxious parent chaperone. There was a girl that had passed out on the bathroom floor after vomiting uncontrollably; another student was in a stall with her friends throwing up, and a third was sitting on the toilet seat being propped up by a group of her posse. I called for help on my radio and called for an ambulance, suspecting the student had overdosed on drugs or alcohol. I quickly assessed that the unconscious girl needed help fast, rolled her over onto her side (my lifeguarding, CPR, and emergency life saver training kicked in), and asked a student to get me a cold water towels. I cleared the bathroom except for the two occupied stalls and the girl's friends and a helper that I enlisted. The unconscious girl was unresponsive but breathing. We carried the ill student into the teacher's lounge I had commandeered as a trauma room. I called her parents using a borrowed cell phone and asked her friend to give me an additional phone number for the girl's parent. I called for the custodians to clean up the bathrooms, "Get me some athletic mats, and give me a garbage can for each student STAT [my psychiatric hospital training]." We laid the student on her side in the staff room until the emergency medical technicians came. I felt as though I was running a trauma unit. I called for another AP. The other two were unavailable—one dealing with a fight in the parking lot, the other dealing with an obnoxious drunk on the dance floor, as I found out later. The other APs had called the police, and I called 911 again for additional ambulances.

I radioed the custodians to establish the boys' bathroom as the girls' and relocate the boys' to the faculty bathroom. I began to wonder if more of this kind of behavior would occur. Then I went into the stall with the student whose head was being held over the toilet by her girlfriend. Two students and I laid this girl sideways on the now-clean but wet floor. Her friends told me that she must have eaten really bad Chinese food that day. (That and a half a pint of scotch on a young stomach might do it.) I designated a student to get everybody's name and phone number and moved this girl into the "trauma center." We did the same with the other student who was sitting on the toilet, holding her head and moaning loudly. I had to call each parent at home (before cell phones were common) and tell them to come to the high school, what was going on, and that we had called for an ambulance for each student. One of the parents screamed at me on the phone that she didn't want her daughter going anywhere. I told her that if I felt it was quicker to save her life, I was putting her in the ambulance, and I did so. I would let the EMTs make the decision. All three of the students went to the hospital by ambulance—I wanted them to check blood/alcohol levels at least, and they did. The other APs had two students each who needed an ambulance and the police.

One parent told me that her child had an accident that resulted in a head injury in soccer that afternoon and that it was the reason her daughter was throwing her guts up and that this child would never take drugs or do alcohol. (Would you even send your child to a dance after a head injury?) This mother angrily wanted to know why I even thought her child had thrown up alcohol. I gently placed her daughter's trashcan with the emesis still in it and told her to take a whiff as I walked away.

I was exhausted after that night when all the students left the dance about twelve-thirty. It had been a long night. Now all the APs had to contact the parents the next day to assess how their little darlings were doing, interview all the witnesses of every student involved in the alcohol fling, arrange for principal's hearings, and then find dates for superintendent hearings and write reports about each incident. All this for a little spring dance to help students socialize?

Let me let you in a little trend today. Students nowadays plan for this dance day far in advance. The fifteen-year-olds don't eat much on the day of the dance, plan a lot of physical activity, bring shots of stuff to one another's houses to "get dressed together," and share whatever they can get their hands on from their parents' cache—substances such as vodka, gin, wine, etc.—and mix it with a little Snapple or Diet Coke to get a buzz. They spray tons of perfume, use breath strips, and put on nail polish and hand and body lotion—whatever is necessary to disguise their high. When they get to the dance, they don't look drunk. After they dance/hop for about thirty minutes, they throw up. It's that simple.

This is what our high school children do before a dance in this country. I once visited a predominant high school on the outskirts of Pittsburgh, Pennsylvania. The AP there told me that they did away with dances to avoid the liability. Now the local YMCA holds dances sometimes. Even the senior prom is held outside of the school district confines, and the parents must pay for security guards themselves. Students are bused from their school directly to the dance. Then there is less chance to pick up alcohol on the way, but they prepare well anyway.

I, however, began to wonder why I had never read about this sort of thing in my educational administration courses. Dirty little secret perhaps?

THE REGENCY

At the top of the educational food chain in New York State is a group of individuals who serve to govern the educational system, along with the commissioner of education, the governor of the state, and many subordinates. They are responsible for the standards of all curriculum taught in New York State from birth until graduation from high school. They even direct the state universities and oversee the private colleges within the state. "Estes gentes y mujeres son muy importante!" Since acquisition of federal money is now tied to some kind of accountability, thanks to No Child Left Behind (NCLB) in the past and the Race to the Top money from the Obama administration, it is imperative that a state continue to show improvement in literacy and mathematics, among several other areas. No gains, no money, unless the excuses are really, really good, and then the regents can determine that a school is in need of improvement or should even be closed.

The list of people who become regents changes according to the political players in the state. State assembly men and women lobby for their friends to achieve such a coveted position. Many of the men and women who serve as regents have earned advanced degrees in disciplines other than education, such as law or business. Few, if any, have ever taught in a public school during their careers. Some have been college professors without the benefit of a teaching certificate from the state they are teaching in themselves, and some have been judges. Many of the regents have never spent more than an hour in a public school. Ask them to document their official time in a public school or a state university, and most will say they have spent little time except for ceremonial duties.

At one time, I aspired to become a regent in Albany, New York, and I began to ask everyone I knew in education, "How do I become a regent?" I had the correct certification to be a school district superintendent, and I had lots of teaching experience—birth to graduate school-age students.

The only answer I received to my questions was, "It's a political appointment." OK. So whom do I call to get on the list? Most people told me I should forget about it. I figured that these "advisors" probably made tons of money, had great offices in Albany, and spent tons of nights in fancy hotels. This was the belief I had until someone told me that the position does not pay.

I guess I lost interest in the regents position as a result of the work required and the zero remuneration. What *would* the motivation be for someone to tackle a position as difficult as administering a whole collection of educational policies, federal mandates, and reform movements without pay? No wonder nothing changes. It doesn't matter if you produce or not for the benefit of the education of the state's youth. It is a voluntary board assigned by political influence. How could anyone expect grass roots movement changes? If the public really knew, OK, Mr. or Mrs. Regent out there, write me a rebuttal.

CSE CHAIR

What is a CSE chair, and why is this important information? A CSE chair is a committee of special education chairperson. I had to be interviewed in my district three times for this position because the title had changed, and the tasks changed slightly. Luckily, the skill set was similar to the elementary support teacher position I had been doing for several years before the change in title. It is a semi administrative position that requires knowledge of special education law and is supposed to be someone who is an advocate for children with disabilities. There is no specific certification required in this state of New York for this position, except most have special education background of some sort. An administrative certificate is not required but desired of the applicants.

It is a position that leads a committee of educators, psychologists, parents, etc., to choose a disability category for educational purposes and construct an individual educational plan (IEP) for a student. The federal law was first developed in 1973 when the Ninety-Fourth Congress passed the Education for All Handicapped Children Act (PL 94-142), an educational offshoot of the 504 mandate that established access to all buildings and civil rights to persons with a disability. Since 1973, the law has been refined and authorized many times, but each state must adopt this federal mandate if they receive any public federal monies.

Well, for many years (ten at least), this was the position I held in this centrally isolated Upstate New York school district with various different titles. I knew and understood the federal laws, have a background in special education (speech pathology), and taught about normal language and literacy development on the college level as an adjunct instructor. I had worked with people with each of the thirteen areas of disabilities and hold a minor in psychology. I had held many other leadership positions, and this, by far, taps into all my interests.

A good day is when I came home and told my husband that only two sets of parents cried during the day at our committee meetings when we discussed someone's child. To tell a parent that their child has a disability has got to be one of the hardest jobs around, except that of a physician who has to tell a parent their child is terminally sick and dying. It tears at your heartstrings because the diagnosis of a disability, such as having a learning disability, could thwart a family's hopes and dreams of having a child that will do well in school and beyond. Their child will need extensive help throughout their educational career. In my experience, many parents also had difficulties in the same way when it came to reading, writing, or math, and they wanted their child to experience more success in school than they had experienced.

I led three teams a week in three different schools, and each time we set out to develop a plan for the student, the special education teacher would most often assume the role of primary literacy or math teacher. What? Isn't that the classroom teacher's job?

The most unfair part of this law is that it separates those children from the rest of the class in order to "shore up" the skills. The children who have the most difficulty with transitions wind up transitioning the most. Even if the student is included, they are oftentimes physically separated in the classroom so their aide, special education teacher, etc., can provide additional repetitive instruction.

This special education law is fraught with good intentions, but the core of the problem stems from socioeconomic factors (even though these factors are supposed to be ruled out) and a cognitive capability not understood by the regents in the state of New York. The fact that 50 percent of students with an IEP in this state don't graduate from high school is not because teachers don't work hard; it is because the shoes don't fit. Today the curriculum is outdated, and no vocational programs diploma exists for many of the students in my state of New York, except for a chosen few. This is just wrong. Those students with high-performance capabilities but lower vocabulary skills are up you-know-what creek for life in New York. If they move to Pennsylvania, they can apprentice with a tradesperson, graduate with a diploma, and get on with life working in a trade. If the student in Pennsylvania changes their mind, the community colleges are designed to fill in the gaps so they can attend a college or university. In New York State, the students who do not have an opportunity to participate in a limited vocational program are just plain screwed.

It took me many years to realize that this must be part of the New York State regent's plan—to keep an underclass of workers in the state. Oh no, how could I say that? Well, someone needs to mow the lawns, dig the ditches, and clean the toilets of the people of New York. If all the students in the state *did* graduate and go on to college, we would be in serious trouble. Without vocational education, except for a small minority, this system guarantees an underclass of workers needed for those dirty jobs no one wants to do. The sad part is that I can tell, with a fair degree of accuracy, whether a child will graduate from a New York State high school based on their performance by the end of second grade. If the student has not learned to decode the words of our language and reads at a grade level, the picture isn't pretty for future success within the educational game.

I spent about four years as an elementary chairperson of special education. The way the position was structured, I worked in three different elementary schools during one week. I had a secretary in the district office to set up the meetings, and my office was located in the central office of the administration building. I was given a laptop and training on the new (now old) IEP Direct computer program. Mondays and Fridays were reserved for paperwork, but we had to be flexible to accommodate working parents. I had two other colleagues doing the same job in the same little windowless office and limited support from the principals whose buildings I was supposed to work in each week. The Response to Intervention movement and differentiation of instruction practices were the key new-wave elements I was supposed to encourage teachers to support.

I am an advocate for the disabled, but not every child with a learning disability wants to take advanced placement calculus, and currently in New York State, we have few other options for students who do not want to attend a college or university, as I have stated. We have a limited vocational program through the BOCES (Boards of Cooperative Educational Services), like a consortium of services for smaller school districts. The problem is, the student needed to be sixteen years old and each district had very few spots. A fourteen-year-old student with a cognitive delay had to wait and apply. In the meantime, until she was sixteen, she would be included in the regular high school regents diploma classes, with modifications. Or she could be in a special education classroom with an emphasis on functional math, reading, and writing skills. Sounds good, but it is not always an appropriate course of study for a child who just wants to work with plants or animals.

I have briefly described the entire special education movement as one with very good intentions but many, many limitations. It is now time to leave "No Child Left Behind" behind and begin to cultivate an option for students to work with their hands at age fourteen, and kids will stay in school longer. Just ask the folks in Pennsylvania or Europe.

ADMINISTRATION HORSE TRADING

When one administrator in a school district has reached his/her peak, has outlived his/her usefulness, or has gone over the edge, then a common practice among the upper echelon of superintendents, directors, boards of education, etc., is to exchange the person with another school district.

"Want a guy to break your union?"

"Got him right here."

"Need a gal to convince the teachers to use a different program?"

"I got her right here."

Need to switch someone because of a quickie in the parking lot with a secretary? Trade him Upstate where the weather is colder and parking lots are not as desirable. The unwritten laws of horse-trading men and women are that you know the horses' strengths, weaknesses, and faults. Your district can no longer tolerate a rude, selfish person, but the district fifty miles away could use such a guy, and you don't have to tell the other district about the weaknesses. Buyer Beware exists in the housing market as well as in the human "desource" game.

So what do you do? Call your buddy, and make a deal. Trade. You need a director; he needs a new place for a principal. What a switch! Just like trading horses.

After all, isn't it for "the good of the children"? So what if the guy/gal that was traded was really lousy? Doesn't matter—just fill the void, and tell him/her to keep their mouths shut, or else . . . The problem with the educational system is that the kids are the least thought of as the administrators do their moving. Many times the feeling is that the further down the line you can get from interacting with kids, the more successful you will be. Yuck. Who wants kids' germs anyway?

So you advance in the system by being traded. Kind of like the NFL—only in this game, the salaries never really get beyond $100,000 a year, which sounds like a lot, but in New York State, it's peanuts if you want to buy a house, have a steady diet including meat, and plan to drive a car worth less than $50,000 *ever* in your lifetime. Protect your pension plan, and you will make it through the game. That is the mantra. Drop out early by taking a job in Florida, and you will be penalized because you will have to pay taxes on that New York *State* pension if you move to any other state in the country. You and your pension are imprisoned in New York. Didn't tell you that in the recruitment interview when you were twenty-one, did they?

I know a human resources director who outstayed his welcome in our liberal town. He was traded and, after a few years, was not offered a position in that area again. What's interesting is that sometimes it takes a few trades before the "system" figures out how bad someone really is and stops the process. "Please resign, or you will be fired."

So if you are bad or too good, you will get traded. Hopefully, it will be to a Long Island, school district so you can live in a small apartment, but get into New York City to see plays and concerts. But if you get stuck in Watertown, New York, well, you just better start investing in long underwear—and good luck trying to get to a warmer place in the state. That's why G—d invented Florida—with an added cost. This is another dirty little secret in public education that no one will ever admit to doing. Not ever.

MONKEY SEES MONKEY DOES

Life in a public school is like a favorite daily soap opera on television. People gossip and people sleep with other people's wives, husbands, girlfriends, and mistresses. Watch out for those annual education conventions, which are breeding grounds for budding love affairs. There have been many administrators who have been known to slink through the lobby early in the morning as they crawl back to their room in time for a shower and breakfast before the seminar. "Walk of Shame."

The community of educators is not that vast, and word travels quickly in hushed tones in the district offices throughout the state. The drama of it all could be acted in dozens of soap episodes like "Days of Our School Lives" or "As the School District Turns." The episodes would shock the general American public.

Many deals are made through these bedroom liaisons. People and positions are exchanged under bedcovers and with various deals in mind. "I'll trade you this resource director if you give me your African American assistant superintendent." By the time of the official job search, it has already been decided who will get what job. This is the result of a "successful" convention. Arriving back home with only a few "scores" is not considered to be good use of a director's recruiting time.

The fact that this practice violates affirmative-action regulations is not often detected and is not often questioned since a "search" will follow the guidelines, *but* the person actually hired will be handpicked.

The problem with this procedure is that it not only shuts out the average person with good qualifications, but that it is a fairly incestuous practice that rotates the same people through the same positions with little impact on the community that the new hires are supposed to be serving. In a sense, the school district in the country or the state does not matter; the person is merely a tool in the tool belt. And they *all* do it. All the headhunters in human "desource" follow these practices, and if they tell you they don't, well, they are fibbing.

The core of the problem is that, although hectic and demanding after a few years, administrator positions can get pretty boring, so why not move up? If you were a good monkey, made nice with the big boys and girls, you might be elevated to the higher parts of the tree, where the fruit is plentiful. Or if you were an antisocial monkey who refused to pay his/her share of the Christmas party dues (even if you were Jewish or Muslim) and won't play the blame game or pet (stroke the egos of) your fellow monkeys, then, well, tough luck. Rotten bananas and banana peels on the bottom of the tree is what you will get. Just do what the older monkeys do—smile, scratch your head, and pretend you are in agreement with the head monkey at all times.

The message here is to pick your path wisely as you ascend to become the top monkey. This is reality, and in the educational administration world, reality bites sometimes.

TECHNO THREATS

It should come as no surprise that with the invention of the portable laptop and the cell phone, students of today's school systems carry around with them many distractions that keep them from focusing on regular, daily schoolwork. What with instant messages on Facebook or Twitter—kids have a tough time just paying attention for an extended period of time. As the techno gadgets buzz, whir, and vibrate, or all three at once, they do serve as reinforcement that the student has friends, are liked, or are important. As distracters go, these toys are the worst in a classroom, and most teachers today have an established policy of "turn them off before walking in the classroom, or they will be confiscated." Parents who contact their children during the school day know it is better to text than to call to avoid interruptions.

These new technological advances in communication have been a real boon to the disabled and to the student who finds it difficult to make friends, but they can also be an associate principal's nightmare. Often the words placed on Face book the night before can have a direct effect on a student's educational performance the next day.

"He was writing shit about me on Face book."

"She wrote that I was a whore at the dance."

"He wrote that I had no life."

"She told her friends I actually liked the guy and did things with him."

These quotes are real and from real high school students this year (2013), and they occurred during regular class time in an AP's office. This means the student was not in the math/English/government class they were supposed to be in during the period. If the United States is experiencing dumbing down of the curriculum, dumbing down of states of grace and manners has already occurred. Television shows that continue to enhance the state of dumbness, like *Jersey Shore* and the *Real Housewives of New York City,* continue to glorify the real reason technology has increased communication—not for information, as many believe (sorry, Al Gore), but to have an extra medium to make each person look better or worse in the game of socialization. Teens spend so much time watching poor role models of behavior on television that asking them to discuss anything else becomes the real challenge of today's educator. If questions about the characters on *Jersey Shore* appeared on the state tests, there would be no problem, but Thoreau and Frost did not have guest appearances, so many of these teens know nothin'.

The really smart teacher of today has to be all-knowing of the culture of *Us Weekly* magazine even more than before in order to relate. The last time an interviewer asked pop culture icons who their favorite author (not Arthur) was or what book influenced their lives was probably during the Sarah Palin fiasco. There are pop-star exceptions that have completed a degree, but the overall concept of knowledge is just not respected. Stereotypes are reinforced when the "guidos" are presented to the students as having little experience with literature.

The ethos of the regular public high school demands that students participate in the fashion and technology trends of the society. If the high school students understood that by dressing and acting the way they do makes them conformists, as opposed to individualists, I often wonder how things would change. For example, the "jeans and T-shirt hanging over the pants" look for boys or the "bra straps hanging out of shirt" look for girls could be considered so old fashioned if some designer made it imperative to tuck shirts into pants (no jeans) and, for girls, showing straps to the public so wrong that it would be considered laughable. OK, Tommy Hilfiger, I challenge you now to change the way kids dress. I usually comment out loud to the student about his "panties" if the pants are hanging so low I can see the design of the underwear. I figured that if they are wearing them so I can see them, I have the right to comment on the color or the fabric. This usually gets a reaction from the student whereupon I have the excuse to say,

"If you don't want comments, pull up your pants and wear a belt." I also comment on girls' bra straps when hanging out, "Nice design" or "Is that from the Victoria's Secret collection?" Technology today allows students to set trends, share ideas faster, and contact their families faster to bring a change of appropriate clothing to eliminate sexual distraction. Is that the real purpose of a teen having a cell phone? Probably not, but all APs know you can get to the parent a lot faster if the kid calls them to bring a belt—and that is a good use of technology. Maybe we need an entire different kind of education. I keep thinking of the television cartoon show years back called the *Jetsons* and the technology they used that we are now just acquiring every day.

THE UTOPIAN SCHOOL DISTRICT

The science fiction I read as a child and as an adult never really had any detailed information about the perfect public school district in the future. Science fiction authors seemed to shy away from predicting how those technological wonders would develop over time. The formal education needed to produce more energy, expend less energy, or build green structures for the housing we will require in the future has never been detailed until recently. Many new charter schools in this country, at least in my neck of the woods, have established curricula surrounding the environment. This is a good thing for so many reasons. Many times it takes a small school movement, like charter schools, for the public education systems to think differently. That is the beauty of being small; you can make changes much more efficiently than a mega monster public school system. My hope is that our regents in New York State would have some discussion planned about the future of education on their agenda next year. Planning for the future will be necessary if we are to keep our children engaged in schools within even the next generation. The dropout rate from our high schools will need to decrease sharply because those uneducated students will be forced to perform menial jobs for the rest of their lives.

In the beginning of our country's formal public education, the one-room schoolhouse was created by each local community, and the students were taught in a mixed-age environment, like today's charter schools, with specific standards that needed to be reached in order to be promoted to the next grade. I could imagine what a futuristic curriculum would look like for grades prekindergarten to the twelfth grade in a public school. Driven by the variation in student learning styles, the educators would be forced into teaching a subject matter in many different ways.

Our universities and colleges producing today's educators have to rethink how they are training teachers and how those teachers will need to teach. For older students, the utopian school would carefully develop a plan of curriculum to suit each student's learning style, interests, skills, and aptitude. There would be math and literacy standards for each level, but students could progress through their personal modules at their own pace using distance learning, standard classroom participation, online coursework, and internships with community professionals. For example, in the utopian school, the high school curriculum would be very different.

A thing of the past is the idea of a concrete building holding students inside, a typical public school these days, as the only place or means of education. Students would be able to learn during the day, afternoon, or evening, depending on their personal curriculum dictums via long-distance learning modules. This would eliminate many of the dropouts today who cannot fit into the "four-year high school, change classes, sit and listen" format of their grandmothers and grandfathers. Some students will take six years, and some will complete all the requirements in three years and head off to another educational institution appropriate to their own goals. The utopian school system would have the following ideas. These are just some thoughts. I know that as a committee, we would be developing many more alternatives.

Materials

The materials in the classroom will be different just as they are totally different from thirty years ago. In most developed nations, chalk has been replaced by PowerPoint presentations just as computers have replaced mimeos (remember *that* word?). School materials develop as technology develops, and curriculum demands changes that support it. Some classes and subjects could be mastered online, just as college students now complete online courses. Benchmarks for each grade could require some modicum of online learning and mastery. Think of a pod developed for the spelling of all words that contain the "*i* before the *e* rule" or an increase in Spanish vocabulary taught in a gamelike context like the app I have on my phone. When it comes to these kinds of course-of-study changes, thinking out of the box is not enough; one must reconfigure the entire box.

Technology

The technology subject matter at the high school level would require the state-of-the-art CAD system, for example, with ties to real architects and engineers. The fabrication of materials would need to be completely revitalized with tools provided by the school district to craft designs in an assortment of ecologically friendly substances. All efforts would be made to educate similar to a real life situation so that building, farming, and engineering projects would be taught by certified teachers who were also proficient in the trades. This would demand constant changes in monies allocated for updated technology and its management. This should be included in budgets as a matter of course, just like personnel expenditures.

The School Year

As mentioned previously, the sacred 180-day farm-based school year schedule of 9:00 AM to 3:00 PM will just have to end. This will cost more for each taxpayer and each district, but in the end, maybe more of our dropout students will not end up in jail, which costs a lot more than extended school days and weeks.

As it is now, our students in the United States attend school much less than students in other developed countries. We need to expand the school day and the school year, but the emphasis would change so that the drudgery of nine-to-three day would look much different. As the curriculum changes, this makes sense, and time out of school, used to practice skills learned in the classroom, becomes more valuable than free time as it is structured today. Some charter schools in New York City approach the school year as a nine-to-five experience with activities as part of the requirement, as should all public schools. Please lessen the amount of busywork homework, and increase practical skills!

In Summary

In the final development of the school in the future, we must examine all areas of the typical child's school day at the prekindergarten to the senior year of high school. As an elementary support teacher, I would register incoming students and screen their language skills, motor skills, and writing skills. I would often say that what we need the most to give to parents on that day is the form our high school guidance department would give to juniors in high school to complete. The form served as a document of the student's accomplishments throughout their school career. The students would need to write their activities, awards, volunteerism, accomplishments, and more. The guidance counselors would use this information to recommend colleges or universities that matched the student and their grades. *All* incoming kindergarten parents should be handed this form so they will know to guide their child to be able to complete each area of the form. The parents should be partners from day one, and in the utopian district, they are an integral part of each child's education.

ARCHITECTURE

Let's start the utopian school district by rethinking the way schools are built. The freedom to design the structure from the ground up with no restriction is a writer's prerogative. However, the practical side of an institutional design has to meet future federal and state curriculum and green standards.

First, all new schools should be constructed with a smaller school population in mind, centrally located by common areas, such as cafeterias, libraries, music facilities, and a sports complex. Shared resources are one of the primary principals of the green movement. If the computer stations, activity areas, and small offices for support personnel are located within a central building, close to the academic areas, then the adult supervision increases during transition times. Offices of school administrators would be located throughout the system so as to become part of the student structures. The concept of a front office where the principal resides would be eliminated in favor of an office within an academic area. Nursing stations are also scattered throughout the various complexes linked together by the Internet and phones. Rooms for copy machines, printers, staff lounges, and toilets for all would also be incorporated into each pod, shared equally between students, staff, and faculty. This increases the amount of verbal and physical interactions between all age groups and helps with an understanding of all aspects of the educational process.

The school complex should be located close to a city center and accessible by public transportation, allowing all involved in the school life to be able to take a train or a bus, ride bicycles, or take a subway to the complex like Frederick Douglas Academy in Harlem, New York City. Think of modern-day airports as the model, where people are directed from one area to the next efficiently with color-coded signs and symbols to introduce common areas. This would help all the people who use the building to find their way and lead to less confusion during the transition times. Schools need traffic studies done just as the transportation systems do to eliminate future blockage problems, which lead to students fighting in a confined space.

Student attendance could be taken as a student swipes his/her identification card when entering the complex. Pertinent information is entered into the central office computer immediately so the student is known to be within the building. Each student would be issued a laptop computer or an iPad, free of charge and theirs to keep, with Internet availability and a printer so that teachers would be able to give assignments, correct assignments, and clarify student questions equally to all students, regardless of economic advantages or disadvantages. This would be the greatest single factor to address compounding issues of race, class, and diversity within the student population and educational equity. No excuses for not being able to complete whatever is assigned.

All too often, the buildings are designed by engineers and architects worried about cost or structure, not concerned if the building itself will be conducive to student learning and student interactions. All one needs to do is to visit a local high school, which was built around the 1960s or 1970s to see that the design itself is outdated. As a result, the structure influences the function, and the students find the unsupervised areas (weak areas) to hide in just as water seeks areas of least resistance. Social problems arise in schools simply because no adult crosses the student's path during the particular time. The building itself will monitor its own heat, electricity, and water, preventing some areas from being overheated or a lack of heat in some areas, like hallways, which tend to remain at a freezing level in the winter. The building would be constructed with garden roofs, solar heating, and all the features of a techno-smart green structure. The savings would be passed on to the taxpayer in the form of lower taxes to homeowners.

Each student assigned to a pod would have a pod leader, similar to the concept of a homeroom teacher but more family inclusive with a team of support personnel available to the student and family. The concept of a pod is where development can occur alongside others equally in small units within the protection of a cover. Think of peas and how they grow. Each pod leader would stay with the student and the family for the entire school experience at the middle and high school levels. The research in education and student outcomes with regard to staying in school until graduation supports the concept that students who identify with specific individuals within a school environment have a better chance of completing a high school degree. This is an important aspect of the utopian school as we recognize that teacher contacts during the day are not enough for many students. Students now need more adult contact (minutes per day) on a daily basis in order to be successful. The behaviors demonstrated by most normal middle and high school pupils do suggest that they need more supervision than previously thought to learn to avoid destructive habits and to learn appropriate behaviors.

Since the early 1960s, many school districts in the United States separated students by age and grade into two distinct subgroups based on the premise of shared resources and learning behaviors of students. However, students in this decade are quite different from students in the past in terms of their social skills and their learning styles. The idea of a middle school starting at grade 6 and ending in grade 8 does not work as well any longer. In addition, grouping students together in this age range guarantees that social factors—because of normal, natural development of humans—can interfere with learning on a daily basis. The years I spent at the middle school level as a teacher, then administrator, have various horrific events cemented in my brain. The daily "He said, she said" referrals indicated to me early on that this large grouping of individuals at this age range needed to be examined.

I propose we reexamine the groupings we have established as the norm and start all over again. First, we need to put the sixth graders back into the elementary school, where they have the opportunity to be the leaders of the school and lessen the chance that they will emulate inappropriate behavior from older students for one more year. This contains them in an environment where previous teachers can help to monitor their behavior and their study habits. I have witnessed many a "moving up" ceremony at the sixth grade level only to be baffled by the fact that many of the students were really not ready to be in an environment that will require constant changing of classes, responsibilities that overreach their developmental brains, and inadequate academic skills to support the variety of learning styles required by all the new academic demands. Any wonder why middle school students often cry by the end of their third day in their new middle school environment. The pressure on them to succeed under the current model is enormous.

The second major change in the utopian school district would be to continue to group students but in more appropriate developmental ways. Middle school would include grades 7, 8, and 9 when students would be placed in the smaller pods during this time period. Each pod will include students from the three grades, the older students available to assist the younger students. Because the pods would be small, like one hundred students, and they would remain in their pod for three years at a time, a family unit develops and additional student support becomes au naturel. High school students would be housed in their pods, grades 10, 11, and 12 in much the same way.

The unique idea of early planning for a student based on their skills, or lack of them, is the third major concept in the utopian school. By the time a student reaches the eighth grade, he/she will be presented with choices to examine during the seventh grade year that would lead them into a professional path, academic path, or a business path. The courses for each path would be devised to meet the New York State standards (for example) but would allow them semivocational training beginning in the eighth grade year. In Europe, this separation of studies occurs when students plan to take various exams that will also determine which high school or vocational school they will attend. In the State of New York now, there is one degree (a regents diploma), so if you have an interest in vocational training, you can maybe, hopefully, perhaps, win a coveted spot in a Boards of Cooperative Education Services (BOCES) program. There are not enough spots for everyone, and you must wait until the age of sixteen. Disinterested fourteen—and fifteen-year-olds wander the halls of our high schools because they do not have an interest in a college-bound degree. How well is this model working? Check the number of dropouts from high schools in the larger cities just in New York State. It isn't working. It must change. According to the members of the industry, we in the United States are not producing enough skilled workers in welding, plumbing, electrical areas, etc. It is easier to get a plumber from Pennsylvania, where they have at least some vocational training. On this continent in the United States, Canada, and Mexico, we had better produce more skilled labor force than we have ever imagined as our infrastructures built by a former skilled labor force continues to crumble. Ever watch the History Channel's shows on the future of the planet? The producers portray scary scenarios about our world in the future but very plausible given environmental signs right now. There will not be a lot of need in a disaster for would-be writers or psychology undergrads but lots of need for medics, construction workers, and crane operators. A regents diploma in the state of New York does not prepare anyway for any of these jobs.

The details of the utopian school demand a closer look at national curriculum and how it is currently taught at each level. In the elementary level, we have learned that reading programs are only as good as the teacher; math programs will always have new ways to get to the same old problems, and science and social studies, while best integrated with reading and math, are always taught only when time allowed. In Sweden, students do not enter formal education until the age of seven, which helps to develop cognitive, motor, language and social skills naturally to prepare students for further rigor. Some elementary schools are incorporating more natural learning techniques such as group learning, hands-on materials, and interweaving of math concepts or reading/writing as extended time frames within the day. These are excellent examples of how we, as humans, learn new things on a daily basis. Elementary schools have always been better about adapting to new ways of teaching or the use of new materials to stir the curiosity. All those Montessori techniques and developmentally appropriate pedagogies will be used at the utopian elementary school. Teachers and administrators will be hired who plan to continue their own developmental learning about their craft through continuing education for adult learners. Qualities in the staff from the beginning of their interviews will insist on the ability to work as a team and to share information. Undermining new programs would not be peer acceptable. Teaching the same way for thirty years would not be a value of the group.

The utopian school would look similar to the schools today, but additional spaces for small groups in which to study, more technology within the classrooms to link them to the world, and increased hands-on curriculum that would lead to practical employment in the future would be created. The utopian school would also have computer stations and distance learning available to families. Student teacher conferences could be via Skype or FaceTime any time the parent is available, not just once in the evening during the fall semester.

However, the middle and high schools need major changes in the manner in which they learn, what they need to learn, and when. Thirteen— to sixteen-year-old children I have always called not formally formed adults. Girls are *so* different from boys at this age. There are many studies and books written about adolescence, and one of my first observations centered on this age group's use of language. As a middle school speech language pathologist, I delivered speech therapy services for students during their school day within their study halls. These were students of normal intelligence but have deficit areas in speech and language. Some had an articulation disorders, but most had very low vocabulary scores, demonstrated by the standardized tests administered in those days. My job was to enhance their vocabulary and help them to understand the lesson so they could participate in class. The boys were the most difficult. Boys at this age tend to grunt or respond with one or two word phrases when asked a direct question. Expanding their vocabulary worked if I used what they knew about what they liked to do and tied it with their science or social studies vocabulary. Hunting, fishing, video games, fooling around, and snowmobiling (central New York) were the only topics they would be interested in despite the curriculum demands. All my efforts centered around getting the boys to practice speaking using new words, to use no slang, and to utter I-don't-knows. I called this developing the language brain of the not-so-fully-formed males. The core curriculum needed to be taught by the regular classroom teachers in a different way because, obviously, the students were not increasing their vocabulary on their own.

The girls, on the other hand, were so chatty they forgot most of what was said and could not pick up the salient items of the topic unless directed to do so. Between the umms, goshes, OMGs, and *likes*, I was lucky if I could understand the English they were speaking. There were no pronoun references, constant double negatives, and the use of whatever words a pop star created that week, which would send me into a tizzy. It became clear to me that if a set of course material at this age was going to stick, it needed to be through hands-on experiences. So I expanded their vocabulary based on the science and social studies curriculum—using as many hands-on materials—and grouped in categories that I called makeup of the day, and they learned more than I could have imagined. My question is, why weren't their regular classroom teachers teaching this way? After a number of situations where I team-taught with another teacher for the year, I began to realize that most curricula at the middle and high school levels were so rushed that students barely had time to breathe. Combine lots of language input at this stage of development in a quick way and the system of changing classes every forty-nine minutes or so—and no wonder it is hard to remember anything. The students are not experiencing as much hands-on learning as they need in order to really apply the concepts.

In the world of today's high school student, having areas in the building to complete projects, speak to teachers in private, or obtain remedial services can be difficult to arrange. Most high schools are not prepared to deal with students who are not interested in playing the education game. Again, the physical plant would change to reflect the need for small-group interaction.

In the utopian school, the students are given choices at the middle school level that will equip them for the world of work in the future, and they can change their minds if they want to because the curriculum is also available at the community college level. The program of study would include many opportunities to observe various professions and intern with the professions during the school year, much like an old-fashion apprenticeship. Then in the summers, the students will learn with the masters as well by spending time with them. Observing people working in various professions not only helps students learn what they are good at, but also, they learn what they don't like to do.

Even though there would be much work to do to create a new school concept, the utopian school could be implemented in a year, given those who believe the underclass should not be perpetuated. This will be the hardest philosophy to change in this country today because of the politics, not the money.

BAR-CODE THE SUCKERS

There are many problems with accountability in a regular public high school that can lead to poor academic performance. Students in some high schools can leave a building, go out to lunch, leave for a work program, or just exit the edifice if they wish. Other schools insist that students sign into an attendance office as they come and go. Some school districts make it mandatory that parents or guardians sign students into school and out of school for appointments in the middle of the day or call the school and inform them of the student's absence. If this procedure is ignored, they bear the harsh insult of receiving an automated call from the attendance department of the school in the middle of the day. Any of these sign-in/sign-out systems are antiquated and require massive human intervention. It would be much more efficient if the students, or their identification cards, were bar-coded.

In the midst of the boom in technology today, we know the location of a bag of potato chips in a large supermarket better than we know where high school students are during the day. The date, the time, and the person selling the chips are all inventoried electronically so that the store knows when to stock additional products. In a regular public high school, we do not always know where the students are within a building, despite a computerized schedule, unless the teachers have recorded their presence by computer or manually when they walk into the classroom and stay for a minimum of eight or nine periods per day. In our centrally located Upstate New York high school at five minutes past the beginning of the class, the recording stops, so the student will not be counted present for the class after that point in time. If every student in the school was required to pass through a bar-code reader when they entered the classroom, we would know immediately if the student was present and the time the student entered the classroom. The teacher would gain at least five minutes of instructional time and would not be interrupted when a student leisurely arrives at the classroom door and saunters in with a swagger. Also, a pattern of tardiness for that day would be electronically reported, and periodic texts or letters home would alert the parent or guardian and the associate principal responsible for discipline for that day.

Time is wasted in public high schools throughout the country when associate principals have to process referrals written by teachers for students who have cut class, were late to class, or have left the building without permission. This behavior interrupts the flow of education and costs taxpayers huge amounts of money each year to police the schools and the school grounds. When I was an associate principal, sometimes the referrals I received from teachers were not processed for several days after they were written or even days after the infractions, making the punishment so far removed from the "crime" of skipping class that it was silly to assign detentions. I once had a freshman student walk through the building every day her parent dropped her off in front of the school. She would spend the day at a local park and then take the bus home *as if* she had been to classes all day. It took weeks before the teachers caught on because she managed to figure out the weaknesses in our system—all she had to do was to show up for one class period and claim she was just late and not counted by the other teachers. A bar-code system would be able to communicate with her parents and the school by the second period of the day if her presence was unaccountable. Eventually, this student was suspended multiple times for insubordination, drug paraphernalia, and leaving the building. Her parents finally wised up, second-mortgaged their home, and sent her to a boarding school in another state.

Students who chose to skip classes often fail those classes and are forced to repeat the course for credit within another semester or in an expensive summer school program. Since the financial crisis of the 2009 and 2010 school years, many states have eliminated high school summer school for credit. This can force a perpetual tardy or skipping student to decide whether to extend their school life beyond the usual four years or drop out and try to earn a GED or general education diploma, which can be harder to obtain than a regular regents diploma unless the student is extremely motivated in the present New York State restricted system. There should be no surprise at all that less than 50 percent of students attending public high school in New York State cities complete a regents diploma. Once a student has cut about a week worth of classes, the student can become overwhelmed with the work required, and they freeze and solve the problem by doing nothing at all.

Imagine the costs saved to New York State taxpayers if students were assigned a bar code to keep track of their movements within the school complex. If the student was automatically recorded not to be in class at the designated time, their parent/guardian would be automatically alerted. ("Johnny has left the building grounds. This is for your information. He will not receive credit for this class, and we are not going to look for him.") This kind of hourly reporting to the parent or guardian would be an associate principal's dream come true. By cutting out the middleman (or woman), parents would not be surprised when Johnny fails the class, and the responsibility for attendance falls on the student and the parent directly. Security guards would no longer have to look for students in the building ("Have you seen Johnny in the bathroom?"), and similar questions would cease because the bathrooms and common areas also require a reading of the bar code for entry and exit. We would know when a student took an extraordinary amount of time in the bathroom. The adoption of a bar-code system might lessen vandalism because of the ability to track who was where and when during the day. We could use the system to track a student's time of entry and exit no matter where they were on the premises. If they left the premises without permission, *zzzziiittt*, an alarm would go off, much like a department store with security tags on clothes and other products.

This bar-code system is doable for a small amount of money, probably less than hiring additional associate principals and security guards. If the students had to wear or bring their ID cards with the bar code to be admitted into the building, then they would pass through various checkpoints, like in an airport, to be able to gain entry into the school building itself. Since bar codes can only be read on an individual basis, students would need to enter all portals by themselves and leave the premises one by one, thus eliminating a horde of students entering at the same time—some may be unknown intruders gaining entry into the building. The bar codes would also inform the central office how many students attended any given day, who went where within the building, and who missed classes and were buzzed when they went outside the electronic fence to grab a smoke. Remember, in this country, we keep really good track of the number of cans of cat food better than we do our most precious commodity, our children.

As for the lack of freedom, well, since when does a sixteen-year-old need more freedom to drive illegally and do drugs with their friends on school time? If the curriculum is boring to that student, obviously, the student's course assignment or school placement needs to change. In the meantime, when Jane and Johnny left the school grounds together, each parent showed up at the school within the hour, they had been called automatically by the Robo call. The system would even assign detention in the school supervision room for the next day, where, by the way, the parent was required to miss work and to volunteer for the day to "mind the ISS store." The parents were required to "volunteer," and they were bar-coded too.

PLACES WHERE I TAUGHT IN A PUBLIC SCHOOL

Here is a list of the physical places in the public schools I was assigned to teach speech and language therapy. As you can see from the list, the environment was not always conducive to learning or toward reaching the goals of the students. The fact that the administrators did not seem to be worried indicated to me that they had no clue what my area of expertise was and why a quiet small place was really the best learning environment. In speech and language therapy sessions, the student has to practice speaking, so I always aimed for a quiet environment so as not to disturb the other students.

- The preschool bathroom.
- The school library.
- The basement of an elementary school near the band room.
- The stage.
- The back of the stage during lunch.
- The cafeteria.
- A shared room with three other reading teachers / speech teachers.

- The back of classrooms, which was fine except for silent reading or writing time.
- The pottery room, which was fine except the days the kiln was fired up.
- The principal's office.
- The front hallway of an elementary school.
- The custodian's closet, which was fine except for the chemicals.
- A small room with a window that did not open and with the heat on constantly, which required a claim with the teachers' union to change, and the school district installed a window that opened.
- The playground, the lunchroom, and the coatroom of an elementary school.
- The regular classroom as a team teacher.
- The boiler room.
- The staff lounge.
- A small closet with no windows.
- An office in the guidance department.
- A shared office with a school psychologist.
- The supply closet for administration.
- The nurses' office.
- The main school office.
- A trailer used as additional teaching space during school construction.
- Others (all the places I have forced myself to forget).

WHAT I'VE LEARNED / CLOSING REMARKS

So after thirty-three years, three months, and three days, I have retired from public education. I've had enough of the challenge and feel as though I have run a good race, played the best game I could, and have succeeded on many different levels.

Have I contributed to society? Yes. Have I changed lives for the better? Yes. Did I follow all the rules? Yes and no. Did I reach my goals? Yes. Yes and yes.

After all the bullshit of dealing with all the ignorant, close-minded administrators, I am happy to report that I actually enjoyed most of my time making a living doing what I said I would do, despite being so baffled by the ignorant decisions I often had to support. Let me say that there are still many problems with the public schools I could not change, but at least, I made significant gains with many, many individual students and families. The fact that so many students and parents were grateful for my expertise is enough.

Listening to a child speak better, working with parents to help with discipline, and forming relationships with students in the community that are lifelong are some of the positives I got out of the positions I had enjoyed over the course of my tenure. Thanks came from many sources, even if not from the people who work in the administrative line or the board of education—clueless as they continue to be about education.

I have learned that Mr. Miller, the very first principal I ever met, created lasting friendships with all his teachers, knew all the children's names in the entire school, and guided practices based on what the teachers told him they needed rather than from big ideas from the top administrators. He trusted his teachers until his death, and for me, he was a good role model.

I have learned that working for someone else is an exercise in humility. A person can be a yes-man or yes-girl for only so long before you lose your own self-worth. I have learned that people at the top of the game are not smarter, not more intelligent, not better people. These folks have just learned how to play the suck-up game much better than I have ever learned to play. Maybe my constitution just begs me to question rather than to go blindly into the night and not ask why, when, and where. I have learned that I am certainly more inquisitive and productive than many of the "adminimonsters" I had to deal with on a daily basis. Fear is not the best way to govern, for sure. It affects the way you do your job on a daily basis. Respect is the way to go through life, and I have always tried to respect the people I work with, no matter how hard it was sometimes or how they could reduce me to tears at home.

I have learned that experiential learning holds the key to the differentiated learning model and that New York State had really better create a vocational education diploma, or we will be so dead in the future. Hands-on learning is the way to go with students who are less than motivated by paper-and-pencil tasks, rote memorization, or a regents diploma that trains you to do nothing but how to apply to colleges.

I have learned that to write well, it is necessary to speak well first. Reading good books helps with both areas. I wish more educators and parents understood that language is the tool that needs to be utilized each day, not television or video games, in order to enhance those skills educators try to reinforce during the measly six hours a day we have to work with children.

I have learned that the public education system needs much more than money to be effective with smaller classes and more opportunity for verbal discourse. Time spent with each student is the best a teacher can give, and if the teacher is supported, then the student will be as well.

When I formally announced my retirement and attended our district retirement celebration at the district office, I was given a clock with an inscription that just demonstrated how ridiculous the whole institution can be. The inscription read "Barbara D. Katz-Brown, CSE Chair." OK. So that was my official *final* job title. But for thirty-three years, I was also a speech therapist, support teacher, assistant principal, academic instructional specialist, summer school principal, chair of various committees, interim administrator, committee on special education chairperson, and more. The fact that my final inscription named only one of my positions indicated to me that the super did not recognize (or care) about the sum total of my contributions. Did I care? Yes. At least they spelled my name correctly.

I will get a pension that I can live with if I am careful. I have time to write, read, and support public education in other ways.

By the way, six months after I received the clock, the name plate fell off. I glued it back on for posterity. Then, I lost the directions for resetting the digital clock when Daylight Savings Time ended. I suppose the district got the last laugh.

AFTERLIFE IN THE PUBLIC SCHOOLS

So after thirty-three years, three months, and three days, I have continued working as a retired person within a centrally isolated school district but in positions that are of my choosing. I have been a board of education—approved substitute administrator for five years since my official retirement. I have served as a substitute elementary principal, substitute associate principal at the high school, temporary English department chair at the high school, and as a superintendent's hearing officer. The district calls, and I go wherever they need me. It is the best of many worlds since I can say, "No, thank you," or I can set my alarm for the next day. The pay is decent for the work, and I am still a member of the school community and the city community as well. In each position, I get to have some influence on the youth of our city, and with my background, it is an easy fit. It may be the best positions I have ever had because I get to try to steer students in the right direction with much less paperwork!

In each substitute position, I have learned even more about the workings of the public school, especially with students who have not bought into the system and do something childlike (they *are* children) and require some sort of disciplinary action. Everything I have written thus far has been reinforced over these last few years. In this state I am in, New York, we do not have enough options for teaching students in the areas of their interests and skills. The core curriculum of today wipes out any kind of practical vocational training. We are losing kids by the minute in our public schools in this state. We are just *not* teaching them what they want to learn and need to learn to be competitive in this technological age. So if they are bored, then the students leave campus, get high, come back onto school grounds, and get sent to a superintendent's hearing after five days of out-of-school suspension. Or they go hunting the night before with their family, leave their knife in their pants pocket, and come to school in the same pants (yuck). They happen to show the knife to their buddy at the lunch table, and a teaching assistant on lunch duty sees it. Suspension, hearing, days out of school . . . and the list goes on and on. Children. Even at age eighteen, the current research suggests that their frontal lobes, used in reasoning, are not fully developed and they do unsafe things. By not fully engaging in their public school experience, many students interrupt their education by getting suspended from school. They get further behind in the classes in which they were already struggling, and the downward spiral begins.

We have great teachers at our high school and many great students who do what they should do every day. They follow the rules. They go to class and do their homework. They are involved in some kind of sport, music, club, cause, or activity. Then we have the *other* students, like the girls who come to school only to show off their outfits, socialize with their girlfriends, and talk trash about other girls. Focusing these students on their studies takes skill and the building of self-esteem. These girls will need to understand what they are learning is relevant to their own lives and futures . . . . The boys at this age like to see how things work (will the lockers catch on fire if ignited?), and they will proceed to discover all that they can to entertain themselves.

I once did a superintendent's hearing where the female student got into a fight with another female because of a comment about the color of her shoe laces. Really? Yes. I suspect my grandmother's high school experience in Canada was vastly different socially in Montreal in 1906, and this kind of nonsense was not tolerated because they all wore the same uniforms and shoes!

For so many students in high school today, school becomes a place to put in your time and do as little as possible but still squeak by maybe. Do we really need to keep disinterested kids in school and make them take classes they care little about? What if we had a system that allowed them to take their classes online or on Saturdays or in the evening? After my life as a tenured professional in the public schools, and now with my experiences as a substitute administrator, I have come to realize that stupidity is doing the same thing over and over again with the same results—not my theory but one that is popular and true about the system we call public schools in this state.

What still amazes me is that most parents have no clue what a typical day is like for their high school student and the pressures they feel. Open-house nights give a parent a feel for the classes their little darlings take, but few parents hang out in the school lunchrooms during school hours or in the hallways or even on school grounds. Not that we as educators want a bunch of parents hanging out all day, but it would be nice if a few of the parents of the troubled kids were directed to be with their child for a few days and see what the climate is in the corridors.

TIPS FOR SURVIVING PUBLIC EDUCATION

The following tips for surviving public education have been developed by me during the course of over thirty years in public education. They are not just meant for the beginning teacher but for the veteran teacher as well. Some of these ideas I picked up while in the Girl Scouts, and some while in the various positions I held.

I tried to practice each of these tips, and they worked for me in every school community in which I worked. I only realized after about my fifth year in the public schools that if the game is going to be played well, it helped to know the rules. Rather than serve these up as rules to be followed, suffice it to say that tips fare better semantically and give the participant more of the option to use them rather than insisting that behavior be dictated by rules. You'll get enough of that anyway in an institution such as public education.

TIPS

1. Approach each day with the attitude that you will learn something new while you are being paid to work.

2. Become really friendly with the custodian at your school, the nurse, and the secretary for they are usually your lifeline to success and happiness.
3. Treat all employees with respect equally and with dignity. It takes all positions, from bus drivers to classroom aides, to make a friendly environment.
4. Become as flexible in the workplace as you can be to accommodate everyone's wants and needs.
5. Don't ever whine about how much work you have to do. Others have just as much. You wanted the job.
6. Verbally encourage your colleagues, and discourage gossip and negative comments about other people.
7. Develop a relationship with your administrator quickly, and keep it ongoing. E-mails about *good* things observed throughout the schools will keep her/him informed and appreciated. It can be isolating at the top of the food chain.
8. Keep your friends close and your enemies closer.
9. Keep taking courses throughout your career to learn as much as you can about public education, and earn additional certifications. It will make you a better teacher and/or administrator.
10. Apply for any and all the positions you want to try, either within your district or in other districts. You never know what the rest of the pool looks like, and you may have a good chance.
11. Interview as many times as you can get an interview. It enhances your communication skills and forces you to keep your résumé up to date.
12. Arrive at school first. You needn't also leave last, but by arriving first, you give the impression of being prepared, which is crucial in any position.
13. Join committees if you want to be involved. Also, you usually get to interact with staff you might not otherwise see during the day. This is good for public relations too.
14. Don't join a clique as if you were in high school. This can alienate another group of people and the administrator. You also lose your individual "voice" when seen as a dissenting member of a group.
15. Dress better than the rest of the staff. Look like a professional who would like to advance in her/his career, if you ever hope to succeed.
16. Go to school functions even if you are exhausted from the week. Parents love to see their child's teacher out and about.
17. Do meet with your administrator as often as you can to let them know how your students are doing and what is working.
18. Finally, smile. It could be worse. You could be looking for a job!

INE • 274-9230 • SGATTINE © GANNETT.COM
ITHACAJOURNAL.COM • TUESDAY, JUNE 18, 2013 • 3A

H.S. grad gaps persist

Big cities, minorities trail statewide rate

By Jessica Bakeman
jbakeman©gannett.com

ALBANY—New York's high school graduation rate last year remained at 74 percent, the same as for those who graduated in 2011 after four years. But the rates were lower for large cities and minorities, the state Education Department said Monday.

The rates for students who are considered ready for college or careers remained low, and the state's "Big Five" school districts saw decreases, particularly Buffalo, the state data showed.

Graduation rates in New York City, Yonkers and Syracuse decreased from 2011, but by less than a percentage point in each case. New York City's graduation rate was 60.4 percent, down from 60.9 percent in 2011; Yonkers' was 66 percent, from 66.2 percent; and Syracuse's was 48 percent, from 48.4 percent.

In Buffalo, the rate dropped by more than seven percentage points, from 54 percent in 2011 to 46.8 percent in 2012. In Rochester, the rate dropped from 45.5 percent in 2011 to 43.4 percent in 2012.

"Graduation rates for our students who entered high school in 2008 are painfully unacceptable," Rochester Superintendent Bolgen Vargas said in a statement. "The fact that the district has predicted a decline this year, because of more stringent Regents requirements and more accurate data, is no comfort to the majority of Rochester families whose children are failing to graduate."

The state tracks how many students are graduating with the skills necessary to succeed in college or in a career. Those numbers were significantly lower than graduation rates.

Statewide, about 35.3 percent of graduates in 2012 were considered ready for college or a career. In Rochester, only 5.8 percent of graduates were college—or career-ready, the lowest of the "Big Five." In New York City, that number was 21.9 percent; in Yonkers, 22.8 percent; in Buffalo, 9.7 percent; and in Syracuse, 7 percent.

Achievement gaps between white students and minorities persist.

About 58.1 percent of black students in New York graduated in 2012 after four years, compared with 85.7 percent of white students. The rate for Hispanic students was lower, at 57.8 percent. Asian students fared better than the statewide average, with about 81.6 percent graduating in four years.

REFERENCE LIST

Blanchard, K., P. Zigarmi, and D. Zigarmi. 1985. *Leadership and the One-Minute Manager: Increasing Effectiveness Through Situational Leadership.* New York: William Morrow and Company.

Berry, B. 2011. *Teaching 2030: What We Must Do for Our Students and Our Public Schools—Now and in the Future.* New York: Teachers College Press.

Calegari, N., and M. Lockington. 2011. *Be Honest and Other Advice from Students Across the Country.* New York: The New Press.

Cameron, J. 2013. *Canaries Reflect on the Mine: Dropouts' Stories of Schooling.* North Carolina: Information Age Publishing.

Cosby, B., and A. Poussaint. 2007. *Come on, People: On the Path from Victims to Victors.* Nashville: Thomas Nelson Inc.

EPF Research Center. 2009. "America's Sorry Graduation Rates." *USA Weekend.* Feb. 26-28, 2010.

Fullan, M. 2003. *The Moral Imperative of School Leadership.* California: Corwin Press.

Gardner, H. 1999. *The Disciplined Mind: Beyond Facts and Standardized Tests, the K-12 Education That Every Child Deserves.* New York: Simon and Schuster.

Gardner, H. 2006. *Multiple Intelligences: New Horizons in Theory and Practice.* New York: Basic Books.

Gladwell, M. 2000 *The Tipping Point: How Little Things Can Make a Big Difference.* New York: Little, Brown and Company.

Gladwell, M. 2008. *Outliers.* New York: Little, Brown and Company.

Karbo, K. 2012. *How Georgia Became O'Keeffe: Lessons on the Art of Living.* Connecticut: Globe Pequot Press.

Kozol, J. 1991. *Savage Inequalities.* New York: Crown Publishers.

Kozol, J. 1967. *Death at Any Early Age.* New York: Plume.

Mahler, Jonathan. 2011. "Reformed School." *The New York Times Magazine.* April 10, 2011. New York, New York.

Matthews, Cara. 2011. "State Education Commissioner Resigning." *The Ithaca Journal.* Friday, April 8, 2011. Ithaca, New York.

Saunders, Sylvia. 2009. "Teacher of the Year Keeps It Real." *New York Teacher.* April 2, 2009. NYSUT, Albany, New York.

Smoot, B. 2010. *Conversations with Great Teachers.* Indiana: Indiana University Press.

Payne, R. 2005. *A Framework for Understanding Poverty.* Texas: aha! Process Inc.

X, Professor. 2011. *In the Basement of the Ivory Tower.* New York: Viking.

ABOUT THE AUTHOR

Barbara Katz-Brown lives in a centrally isolated small city in New York State with her husband, Steve, a jazz guitarist and former director of the jazz studies program at Ithaca College. She has been working in the same public school district for about forty years in a variety of positions. Her hobbies include painting, traveling, and being a jazz musician's wife. After years of seeing how things could change for the better for students within a public school district in the United States, she started writing about the absurdities in practices she found in and throughout the system. This book is a collection of essays written over time spent in the public schools.

Barbara D. Katz-Brown, MS, CCC-SP, SDA

Certification and licenses: Bachelor of science (Ithaca College, Ithaca, New York); master of science (Ithaca College, Ithaca, New York); school district administrator (SUNY Cortland, Cortland, New York) (permanent); New York State Certification as a teacher of the speech and hearing handicapped (permanent); New York State License as a speech-language pathologist; Certificate of Clinical Competence in speech pathology, American Speech-Language-Hearing Association.

Positions held: Speech-language pathologist, Pre-K-12; assistant/associate principal, middle and high school; summer school Title 1 and ESOL principal; elementary support teacher; committee on special education, chairperson; substitute elementary principal; substitute associate high school principal; interim high school English department, chairperson; superintendent hearing officer; and adjunct instructor at the college level (Ithaca College, State University of New York College at Cortland, Tompkins Cortland Community College).

INDEX